Understanding Olympic Ideals

ALSO FROM PARNASSOS PRESS

Olympic Philosophy: The Ideas and Ideals behind the Ancient and Modern Olympic Games
Heather L. Reid, 2020

Conflict and Competition: Agōn in Western Greece
Eds. H.L. Reid, J. Serrati, and T. Sorg, 2020

Athletics, Gymnastics, and Agōn in Plato
Eds. H. Reid, M. Ralkowski & C.P. Zoller, 2020

Pindar in Sicily
Eds. Heather L. Reid and Virginia Lewis, 2021

Aretē in Plato and Aristotle
Eds. Ryan M. Brown and Jay R. Elliott, 2022

Ageless Aretē
Eds. Heather L. Reid and John Serrati, 2022

Body and Soul in Ancient Greece and Rome
Eds. J.R. Gatt, S. Newington, and M. Senkova, 2024

Ancient Olympic Philosophy: Sport, Athletes, Excellence, Education, Women, Beauty, Peace
Heather L. Reid, 2025

Understanding Olympic Ideals

Rafael Mendoza & Heather L. Reid

First Printing: 2026
ISBN: 978–1–942495–819 (paperback)
ISBN: 978–1–942495–826 (hardcover)
ISBN: 978–1–942495–833 (ebook)

Parnassos Press
Fonte Aretusa Organization
Dakota Dunes, South Dakota USA
www.fontearetusa.org

Cover illustration: Herm from the Panathenaic Stadium in Athens, photograph by Heather Reid, printed with permission of the Hellenic Olympic Committee, all rights reserved.

To Hans Lenk
Olympian and Philosopher
1935-2024

Acknowledgments

The authors are primarily indebted to the many participants in various sessions at the International Olympic Academy with whom they have lived these ideals in the classroom, on the playing field, and over coffee in the Academy bar. For their comments and suggestions on the earlier drafts of this book, we also thank Georgios Mouratidis, Tarik Orliczek, Nelson Morales Paez, and Sarah Teetzel.

Table of Contents

Note on the use of sources

To maximize readability, we have modified our use of traditional scholarly conventions.

We do not include footnotes or in-text citations of secondary works. Instead, sources mentioned in the text can be found in a list of references at the end of each chapter. An annotated bibliography of recommended readings in Olympic Studies is provided at the end of the book.

Pierre de Coubertin's writings are identified in-text by the original year of publication, even though most of them come from the volume *Olympism: Selected Writings*, edited by Norbert Müller and published by the IOC in 2000. Essays from this book are referenced as "In Müller, ed. 2000" with the relevant page numbers.

Ancient sources, such as Homer and Plato are not cited in the text or listed in the bibliography, but proper citations can be found in the secondary sources and there is a glossary of ancient Greek terms in the appendix.

Official IOC publications such as the *Olympic Charter* do not appear in the reference lists or bibliography, though key texts from the IOC website are quoted in the appendix. The most important of these, the Fundamental Principles of Olympism, is reproduced in the following pages.

Fundamental Principles of Olympism

From the Olympic Charter of February 3, 2026

1. Olympism is a philosophy of life, exalting and combining in a balanced whole the qualities of body, will and mind. Blending sport with culture and education, Olympism seeks to create a way of life based on the joy of effort, the educational value of good example, social responsibility and respect for internationally recognised human rights and universal fundamental ethical principles within the remit of the Olympic Movement.

2. The goal of Olympism is to place sport at the service of the harmonious development of humankind, with a view to promoting a peaceful society concerned with the preservation of human dignity.

3. The Olympic Movement is the concerted, organised, universal and permanent action, carried out under the supreme authority of the IOC, of all individuals and entities who are inspired by the values of Olympism. It covers the five continents. It reaches its peak with the bringing together of the world's athletes at the great sports festival, the Olympic Games. Its symbol is five interlaced rings.

4. The practice of sport is a human right. Every individual must have access to the practice of

sport, without discrimination of any kind in respect of internationally recognised human rights within the remit of the Olympic Movement. The Olympic spirit requires mutual understanding with a spirit of friendship, solidarity and fair play.

5. Recognising that sport occurs within the framework of society, sports organisations within the Olympic Movement shall apply political neutrality. They have the rights and obligations of autonomy, which include freely establishing and controlling the rules of sport, determining the structure and governance of their organisations, enjoying the right of elections free from any outside influence and the responsibility for ensuring that principles of good governance be applied.

6. The enjoyment of the rights and freedoms set forth in this Olympic Charter shall be secured without discrimination of any kind, such as race, colour, sex, sexual orientation, language, religion, political or other opinion, national or social origin, property, birth or other status.

7. Belonging to the Olympic Movement requires compliance with the Olympic Charter and recognition by the IOC.

Introduction

Ideals matter for the Olympic Games. In fact, ideals are exactly what make them special. Olympic ideals represent aspirations, and the Olympic Charter, the guiding document of the Olympic Movement, outlines its aspirations for personal and social improvement in the Fundamental Principles of a philosophy called Olympism. These ideals are what set Olympic athletes apart, they set Olympic sports apart, and they set the Olympic festival apart—in a way that gives all of these things greater value than their non-Olympic counterparts. In short, ideals are what make something "Olympic," and these ideals haven't changed substantially since their inception in ancient Greece.

Most people know that the history of the Olympic Games begins in Olympia, but few realize that the philosophy called "Olympism" also has its roots there. To understand the ideals that make things "Olympic," we need to look back to the ancient past and the 19th-century revival of the Games, but also forward to the future and, most importantly, to the present to find the Olympic ideals that existed in the past and will endure into the future.

This book attempts to explain Olympism as the "philosophy of life" that the Olympic Charter declares it to be by engaging with the ideas of ancient Greek thinkers like Plato, modern revivalists like Pierre de Coubertin, and contemporary philosophers of sport—as well as the many critics of the Olympic Movement.

A philosophical vision of sport inspired by the archaeological discoveries at Ancient Olympia in the 19th century revealed its educational potential to people like Coubertin, who, in turn, sought to shape the development of modern sport to serve personal and social ideals. More than a century after the revival of the Olympic Games, a fresh encounter with its philosophical ideals is needed to revive sport's ability to address the social challenges of today and tomorrow.

In chapter one, we begin this encounter by asking what makes the Olympic Games special, arguing that it is the ideals that underpin them. Practically speaking, the sports in the Olympic program follow the same rules, use the same equipment, and involve the same people as world championships. Perhaps the Games are bigger, more international, and better covered by the media, but what makes a sports festival "Olympic" are the ideals that they serve and the atmosphere those ideals create.

We understand Olympism to be a philosophy of life grounded in personal, interpersonal, and community ideals—all of which are promoted by the Games. The reality of modern life and sport repeatedly falls short of Olympic ideals, but it is the orientation toward and striving for ideals that makes things "Olympic." The ancient Games were religious, founded on an awareness of human imperfection and the struggle to become more like a god. For Plato, coming to understand moral ideals like courage and justice was the basis for becoming a better person. Being Olympic, first of all, means recognizing and understanding ideals, and then orienting oneself toward their realization.

Olympism centers on a personal ideal of excellence that is exemplified by the athlete. To be sure, elite athletes pursue excellence in their sports, but Olympism's idea of excellence reaches beyond sport to describe a moral disposition aimed at constant self-improvement. The ancient Greeks had a concept called *aretē,* which came to refer to the excellence mortals could achieve through their own efforts. Heroes were the models of *aretē,* and athletes emulated heroic actions in sport.

Athletic excellence is not identical to personal excellence, however, and some would say that elite sport fails to express or even discourages the "balanced whole of body, will, and mind" extolled by Olympism in its first fundamental principle. The personal ideal of excellence is what makes an athlete Olympic, but ensuring the compatibility of athletic and personal excellence is a challenge in the contemporary sports environment.

The Olympic Games add something special to athletic contests, something called the "Olympic spirit," which is described in the fourth Fundamental Principle of Olympism as "mutual understanding with a spirit of friendship, solidarity and fair play." In other words, Olympic sport exemplifies an interpersonal ideal that may be summarized as respect.

Like excellence, this is to be understood as a moral disposition cultivated through sport, even though it is not obvious how athletic competition promotes it. In the ancient Games, a religious atmosphere emphasized people's common humanity and motivated their cooperation. Coubertin hoped to capture that religious sentiment with an enlightened practice of sport capable of transcending the superficial differences that divide people in modern society.

The logic of sport pushes competitors to treat each other as equals: they share a common starting line and are treated equally under the rules—this basic level of respect is needed to make the activity possible. Yet, the modern sportive atmosphere often fails to foster respectful attitudes within competition, encouraging players to see opponents merely as obstacles to their personal success.

The Olympic Oath, in which participants promise to respect one another and sport itself, enhances awareness of the respect embedded in sport and gives rise to an atmosphere imbued with Olympic spirit that inspires gestures of friendship and fairness not only among competitors, but among everyone at the Games.

The Olympic Movement is characterized in the third Fundamental Principle of Olympism as encompassing "all individuals and entities who are inspired by the values of Olympism." In other words, it is a community based on shared ideals that embraces a global vision represented by the symbol of five interlaced rings. This community vision is no less idealistic than the other values, but it should not be imagined as a political achievement; rather, it promotes the moral disposition of (international) friendship.

The ancient Games were not international in the sense that the modern Games are, but their ability to bring diverse groups together helped to generate the very idea of a unified Greek community. This coming together required a major effort to set aside political conflicts called *ekecheiera,* but the peaceful gathering generated a new sense of community. The Olympic Movement should be seen as a community that transcends political differences, and the Olympic festival exemplifies this international community united by ideas.

The modern Olympic Movement does not exist for the sake of sport; rather, sport facilitates the promotion of Olympic ideals because, as we will show, those ideals are encouraged by the logic of sport. The goal of this book is to explain that philosophy in terms of its enduring ideals, which align with the official Olympic values of excellence, respect, and friendship.

Our account is not "official," however, nor do we take it to be definitive. In fact, scholars rightly criticize the International Olympic Committee (IOC) for failing to capture the moral richness of Olympism by reducing it to three core values, excluding key ideals such as justice, equality, and peace. Our aim in this book is to interpret excellence, respect, and friendship in an expansive way that does not exclude wider commitments or alternative perspectives. By engaging with ideas and perspectives from ancient Greece, Pierre de Coubertin, and interdisciplinary sport studies, we seek to initiate reflection on and discussion of Olympism as a living philosophy able to guide the activity of everyone connected with or simply inspired by Olympic ideals.

I

What Makes the Olympic Games Special?

The Power of Ideals

There is something special about the Olympic Games. You can go to the world championship in almost any Olympic sport, the world badminton championship, for example, and find the same athletes, the same uniforms, the same equipment, the same rules and officials, maybe the same venue. You might even find gold, silver, and bronze medals, national flags and anthems, opening and closing ceremonies—but it is just not the same. The feeling isn't the same, the public interest is much less, the ticket prices are lower, the economic potential is modest, and the social impact of the event is accordingly limited.

Admittedly, world championships include only one sport while the Olympic Games include many, but other multi-sport festivals, no matter how closely they imitate the Olympic Games, are just not the same.

Why not?

What do the Olympics have that others lack?

Our answer to these questions is their philosophy—a philosophy that reaches back to ancient Greece, is embedded in sport, gets revived in the late 19th century, and continues to guide the Olympic Movement today. The philosophy is called Olympism, and its "Fundamental Principles" are printed near the beginning of the Olympic Charter. These principles are idealistic; they represent social aspirations that have personal, interpersonal, and communal dimensions.

The Charter also states that "Modern Olympism was conceived by Pierre de Coubertin," a statement that opens the door to an Ancient Olympism and a Future Olympism as well. It is worth asking, however, how ancient Greek ideals can give rise to modern Olympism and endure in the future? And, most importantly, how can those ideals be translated and transferred into the practical realities of the Olympic Movement?

Paradox: Idealism versus Practicality

We understand the philosophical ideals that underpin Olympism to be eternal and unchanging, even though the practical reality of the Olympic Games has changed drastically since ancient times and will continue to change in the future. How can something eternal guide something that's always changing? This is a paradox, which is appropriate since the ancient Greek philosophy that inspires Olympism is full of them.

Paradoxes are seeming contradictions that eventually make sense once our understanding reaches a higher level. The philosopher Socrates, for example, embodies the paradox of wisdom—he is said to be wise because he knows that he doesn't know. On the face of it, this is contradictory: how can you be wise if you don't know anything? Once we realize, however, that believing we already know things prevents us from learning, we begin to understand that by admitting we don't know, we can gain the open-mindedness necessary to learn—in short, to become wise.

To understand Olympism as a philosophy, we must engage with challenging paradoxes, the first of which is embodied in the official mission of the IOC, which is described in the Olympic Charter as "to promote Olympism throughout the world and to lead the Olympic Movement." It is paradoxical because leading the Olympic Movement—including but not limited to the organization of the world's foremost multi-sport event—is practical, a series of concrete actions that take place in material reality. But Olympism is idealistic, a set of ethereal perfections that exist in the realm of thought.

Our individual understandings of these perfect ideals, furthermore, are persistently imperfect and require constant clarification. How can people in the Olympic Movement be practical and philosophical at the same time? How can athletes, coaches, officials, managers, committee members, marketers, journalists, and everyone else under the Olympic umbrella perform their real-world jobs in an Olympic way? After all, the Charter describes the Olympic Movement as "the concerted, organised, universal and permanent action [...] of all individuals and entities who are inspired by the values of Olympism."

The paradox is resolved by understanding that the philosophy of Olympism functions as a guide for the Movement's activities, much like a national constitution or a corporate mission statement. The Olympic Charter claims to govern "the organization, action and operation of the Olympic Movement," by acting as a "basic instrument of a constitutional nature" that "sets forth and recalls the Fundamental Principles and essential values of Olympism."

This means that the Fundamental Principles of Olympism printed at the beginning of the Charter are not just a bunch of pretty words, a kind of poem to enjoy before we read the serious part. On the contrary, they articulate the overarching ideals meant to generate the specific rules and practical activity of the organization. Thus, the success of the Olympic Movement depends not on medals, profits, publicity, market share, or even world records—but rather on inspiring individuals, inside and outside of the Movement itself, to live up to and serve the ideals of Olympism.

Ancient Greek Idealism

To understand how ideals are supposed to guide practice, a famous theory from ancient Greek philosophy is very helpful. Plato's "theory of forms" takes ideas to be more "real" than reality because they are eternal and unchanging, whereas practical reality changes constantly. Nevertheless, our intellectual apprehension of ideals allows us to use them as standards and guidelines for our actions in the world. This can be illustrated with the example of a geometric figure like a circle. We know, theoretically, the "ideal" or "perfect form" of a circle: it is a plane figure in which every point on the circumference is equidistant from the center. But when I go to the chalkboard and try to draw a circle in reality, it is always an imperfect imitation of the "ideal" circle. Maybe with some special tools and a lot of practice, I can come closer to drawing a perfect circle, but it is understood that the circles we draw in the world can only be approximations of the ideal. What our understanding of the ideal circle does is to act as a model and guide for the circles we draw, and we strive to get those circles as close as we can to that idea of perfection.

According to Plato, the same dynamic applies to moral concepts like excellence and fairness. He thinks that perfect ideals of humanity and of community exist, but not in the real world. They are to be found in a realm of ideas accessed through thought, and moral people must make an effort to understand these ideals so they can use them as a guide to improve themselves and their world.

This is easier said than done, of course, and the Platonic model for moral education resembles athletic training. Often set in gymnasiums, the place associated with the training of citizens, Plato's Socratic dialogues describe youths wrestling with ethical ideas like courage, justice, or discipline in the effort to achieve an understanding that will prepare them to act virtuously—a kind of moral fitness called *aretē*. The model derives from ancient sport in which athletes strove to emulate the feats (*athloi*) of heroes. The essential point is that awareness of our imperfection with respect to an ideal motivates the struggle (*agōn*) to improve. The Olympic Games (*Olympiakoi Agōnes*) were one among many manifestations of that struggle.

This model of practical improvement through ideals begins by trying to understand them philosophically, but results in real-world activity—it is not a purely theoretical exercise. Platonic idealists neither ignore reality nor confuse it with the ideal; they know the real world is persistently imperfect. But they are inspired and guided by their understanding of ideals to improve reality.

This way of thinking normatively, i.e., about how things *ought* to be, contrasts with sciences that operate descriptively, i.e., by aiming to describe how things actually are. Platonic idealism can be understood as a method, that is, a path to follow, characterized by rationally understanding the ideal form of social practices while looking critically at their realities. Idealism is not naïve or utopian, but a rational and achievable aspiration that acknowledges the imperfections of our present condition.

Modern Olympic Idealism

It makes sense that the modern Olympic Movement is guided by an ancient Greek style of philosophy, not just because the Games originated in Olympia, but also because Coubertin was knowledgeable about and inspired by ancient Greek ideals. Like Plato, he was an educational reformist who saw in sport an opportunity to equip youth with the moral dispositions needed to confront the political challenges of his time.

The cultural and historical context of 19th-century France was clearly different from that of 4th-century BCE Greece, but Coubertin's idealism looked beyond his particular place and time toward practices that could transcend the kind of social misunderstandings that were causing wars. In fact, Coubertin travelled to England and the United States to observe programs in which sport was able to produce "strong wills and upright hearts at the same time as robust bodies." (1890). These "upright hearts" and "strong wills" correspond to the functional moral dispositions trained in the ancient Greek gymnasium.

When he founded the IOC, Coubertin claimed to be reviving the Olympic spirit of Classical times by restoring its philosophical principles. He also had practical and educational aims similar to those of contemporary peace organizations. With sports as the principal means, Coubertin believed that ancient Greek educational ideals could be "transformed and widened by the internationalism and the spirit of democracy which distinguish the present age" (1935). It is no surprise that such an ambitious and idealistic project caused Coubertin to be "looked upon as a dreamer full of illusions" (1935), but he believed the Greek ideals were adaptable. This is manifested clearly by the Fundamental Principles of Olympism, which, though modified continuously, retain the unmistakable imprint of Coubertin's idealism.

It is obvious from modern Olympism's first Fundamental Principle that it is an idealistic philosophy in the ancient Greek style:

> Olympism is a philosophy of life, exalting and combining in a balanced whole the qualities of body, will and mind. Blending sport with culture and education, Olympism seeks to create a way of life based on the joy of effort, the educational value of good example, social responsibility and respect for internationally recognised human rights and universal fundamental ethical principles...

The goal of modern Olympism (and therefore the Olympic Movement) is equally idealistic:

> The goal of Olympism is to place sport at the service of the harmonious development of humankind, with a view to promoting a peaceful society concerned with the preservation of human dignity.

The definition and goal of Olympism serve as philosophical ideals that guide the Olympic Movement. These are not and never will be descriptions of practical reality, but they are realistic enough to provide the Movement with direction and motivation. They are meant to guide the activities of Olympic organizations by articulating their ultimate purpose and objective. In light of this fact, the success of Olympic institutions lies not in athletic victory, as many might think, but in their ability to promote Olympic ideals.

How sport serves Olympic ideals

It should be underlined that the Olympic Movement does not exist to serve sport; rather, sport serves Olympic ideals. This idea may seem to be at odds with some philosophical claims about sport, specifically that it is autotelic, i.e., an end in itself that should not be used to achieve "external" goods like fame and fortune. The ancient Greeks did not share this view; for them, sport was a means to various religious, political, and educational ends.

Modern Olympism, like its ancient version, is not so much a philosophy of sport but a philosophy of what can be achieved through sport to better humanity. The goods it tries to achieve are not medals or records, much less profit or sponsorship deals. They are personal, interpersonal, and community ideals that can be aligned with the IOC's official Olympic values of excellence, respect, and friendship.

Arguably, these ideals are embedded in the structure of Olympic sports, which have evolved since ancient times with the intention of instilling and evoking certain character traits, which Ancient Greek philosophers called "virtues" and modern ethicists call "moral dispositions." These are essentially trained conditions of human beings (not unlike athletic fitness) that enable the performance of ethically laudable actions.

Olympism's personal ideal is a conception of excellence that is exemplified by the Olympic athlete. Olympism's interpersonal ideal of respect, which indicates how we should treat one another, is exemplified by Olympic sport—that is, by the principles embedded in the structure of sport and an attitude of fair play that reflects an understanding of the activity. Third, Olympism's community ideal of (international) friendship is expressed by the Olympic rings, which evoke the bonds that participants from different nations cultivate during the sports festival. Taken together, these three ideals constitute the basis of Olympism, which historian David C. Young characterizes as "the pursuit of individual human excellence in the context of international brotherhood and goodwill toward men."

The values of the Olympic Movement arise from those of sport itself; indeed, experiencing sport as a participant or a spectator can foster the moral dispositions praised in Olympism—and not by coincidence. Modern philosophers of sport associate excellence, respect, and friendship with the structure of sport itself. For Robert Simon, sport is a "mutual quest for excellence through challenge." Paul Gaffney argues that athletic competition fosters respect by generating a sense of interdependency, reciprocity, and mutual understanding. Sports also cultivate friendship among groups since they are inherently communal activities which, as R. Scott Kretchmar observes, form "testing families." Athletes identify themselves as gymnasts, swimmers, cyclists, etc., in a way that transcends national, ethnic, or cultural differences. As long as the basic structure of Olympic sport remains constant over time, it remains potentially productive of the moral dispositions needed to promote its philosophical ideals.

The torch and the flame

Olympism's link with ancient Greek idealism is symbolized by the Olympic flame that oversees the Games after having been ignited among the ruins of ancient Olympia and carried to the host city in a cross-country relay. Historically, the torch relay was not part of the ancient Olympic Games, but philosophically it represents their connection with ancient Greek ideals. In Greek mythology, fire was a gift from Prometheus, who stole it from the gods and passed it in a fennel stalk to humanity in order to elevate their lives above mere survival. In ancient Greek religion, sacred flames were kept to light sacrificial fires, and athletic contests were sometimes used to decide who would have that honor. At Athens' Panathenaic Games (6th c. BCE – 4th c. CE), a torch relay for teams from various neighborhoods was run from an altar at the site of Plato's Academy to the top of the Acropolis, where the winner ignited the sacred flame.

The 19th-century revivalists did not introduce torches or cauldrons into the modern Games, but Coubertin spoke metaphorically of a torch containing the Olympic spirit as early as

1912, and the poet Kostis Palamas, who wrote the Olympic Hymn sung in the ceremonies to this day, clearly associated ancient Olympic ideals with light and fire. The Hymn's first stanza demonstrates this:

> O Ancient immortal Spirit, pure father
> Of beauty, of greatness and of truth,
> Descend, reveal yourself and flash like
> lightning here,
> Within the glory of your own earth and
> sky.

It wasn't until 1924 that an actual cauldron graced the Olympic stadium in Amsterdam, and the practice of igniting a flame in ancient Olympia and bringing it by torch relay to the Games was inaugurated for the Berlin Games of 1936. That year, Coubertin's message to the athletes was to "remember the fire which, lit by the sun's rays, has come from Olympia to lighten and warm our times. [...] Be careful to keep the sacred flame alive." Like the Fundamental Principles of Olympism, and other rituals with ties to ancient Greece, the Olympic flame serves as a guiding symbol, illuminating the values and aspirations of the Olympic Movement.

Today, it is the local Organizing Committee of each Olympic Games that orchestrates the flame's arrival, but the lighting of the flame from the rays of the sun at Olympia and its initial journey through Greece are under the stewardship of the Hellenic Olympic Committee. That illustrates the connection between the modern Games and ancient Greek ideals, and it ensures that the religious heritage of the ceremony is treated with the proper decorum. In fact, spectators are not allowed to witness the actual ignition of the flame in the sanctuary; rather, they wait in the stadium for the flame to be brought forward in a choreographed procession. The ceremony begins with an invocation to the God Apollo, which reads:

> Sacred silence
> Let the sky, the earth, the sea and the
> winds sound.
> Mountains fall silent.
> Sounds and birds' warbles cease.
>
> For Phoebus, the Light bearer King shall
> keep us company.
> Apollo God of sun and the idea of light
> send your rays and light the sacred torch
> for the hospitable city of…[host city]
> And you Zeus give peace to all peoples
> on earth and
> wreath the winners
> of the Sacred Race

The philosophical idealism of ancient Greece is present not just in the Fundamental Principles of Olympism, but in a variety of symbols and rituals that communicate its ideals.

Critics and challenges

Often, the reality of sport as practiced in the real world falls well short of Olympic ideals; in these cases, the ideals provide a basis for recognizing and battling the corrupting forces. Throughout the ancient and modern history of the Olympic Games, the philosophical ideals of Olympism have been routinely ignored and repeatedly violated. In ancient times, examples of corruption included bribery, violence, and various forms of exclusion. In the modern era, violations persist in issues such as doping, violence, judging scandals, and various forms of discrimination. Beyond the field of play, critics observe how governing bodies and organizing committees have engaged in anti-Olympic practices, including bribery, militarization of host cities, forced displacement of citizens to build Olympic venues, and exploitation of the Games to advance personal and political agendas.

It is important to criticize the many aspects of reality that fall short of Olympic ideals and the values of excellence, respect, and friendship that the Movement professes to uphold. Such failures represent challenges to do better in the future; to push Olympic reality closer to these ideals. But we should also acknowledge our limitations in addressing them.

First of all, failures might reflect flaws in our understanding of the ideals themselves. It is not easy to make sense of Olympic ideals when reality persistently diverges from them; we have to make an effort to reflect on them and find ways to open up possibilities for better future scenarios. Secondly, we must recognize the limitations of our means. Recently, the IOC added the phrase "within the remit of the Olympic Movement" to the Fundamental Principles of Olympism. This disclaimer does not diminish goals such as promoting respect for ethical principles, but it shows that the Movement does not expect to bring them to fruition singlehandedly.

No complex ethical theory is needed to condemn the abuses listed above; it is enough to recognize that they do not align with the Olympic ideals stated in the Charter. Ideals, as Plato taught us, exist separately—they are eternal and never-changing, as compared to the ever-changing reality of the Olympic Games. The challenge for everyone involved in the Movement is to examine that reality critically and change it in a way that better aligns with those ideals—starting at home.

We should try to direct all of our organizational, managerial, and athletic actions toward the goals of Olympism. This is not an easy task, since competing interests have pushed many in the Movement to prioritize power, profit, market expansion, sponsorship, medals, and records over the personal, interpersonal, and community ideals the Movement is meant to promote. Yet, if we reframe our view of the Games by placing the Fundamental Principles of Olympism at the forefront, we may come to understand the ideals that provide their foundation. Then, we can act to help Olympic ideals find realization in practice.

Conclusion

Ultimately, what makes the Olympic Games special is their philosophy and the ideals embedded within it. Since Olympism is a philosophy of life, furthermore, people who are part of the Olympic Movement on the basis of being inspired by those ideals are called upon to "live" Olympism at some level. Just what this means will be discussed in the following chapters, but for now, let us point out that Olympism as a philosophy of life has more to do with *how* we live our lives, on the moral dispositions we express in our activities, than the types of activities themselves.

Olympism is a flexible philosophy, but it is also idealistic, and in order to know how to live Olympically, we have to understand its ideals as best we can—even when they seem frustratingly vague. Paradoxically, however, the vagueness of Olympic ideals enables them to guide a diverse international movement. Olympism offers ideals capable of providing common ground to a diversity of people without being vacuous. Let us try to understand them together.

Questions for reflection and discussion

1. If sports are supposed to serve Olympic ideals, are some sports more "Olympic" than others? Explain how your favorite sport serves Olympic ideals.

2. What are the goals of your country's National Olympic Committee (NOC)? Do they reflect the ideals Olympism?

References

Coubertin, P. (1890). Transatlantic Universities: Conclusions. In N. Müller ed. 2000, *Pierre de Coubertin 1863-1937 - Olympism: Selected Writings* (pp. 99-103).

Coubertin, P. (1935). The Fundamentals of the Philosophy of the Modern Olympics. *Olympic Review* 56 (1956): 52-54.

Coubertin, P. (1936). Message at the close of the Berlin Games. In N. Müller ed. 2000 (pp. 519-520).

Gaffney, P. (2015). Competition. In M. McNamee & W.J. Morgan (Eds.), *Routledge Handbook of the Philosophy of Sport* (pp. 287-299). Routledge.

Kretchmar, R. S. (2018). The nature and value of sporting tests and contests. *NYLS Law Review*, 63(2), 219 - 233.

Simon, R. L. (2014). Theories of sport. In Cesar R. Torres, *The Bloomsbury Companion to the Philosophy of Sport* (pp. 83-97). Bloomsbury.

Young, D. C. (1998). Further thoughts on some issues of early Olympic history. *Journal of Olympic History*, 6(3), 29-41.

II

What Makes Olympic Athletes Special?

The Personal Ideal of Excellence

Olympism is a humanistic philosophy founded on a personal ideal that is exemplified by the figure of the Olympic athlete. But that doesn't mean it is confined to sport. If you ask a diverse group of people to name their ideal Olympian, you will get an even more diverse set of examples: there will be women and men, people from different ethnic groups, athletes in every sport, from every continent, of all sizes and shapes, champions and also-rans. You might also make a separate list of athletes who competed in the Games and even won medals, but fall well short of Olympic ideals.

This philosophical exercise reminds us that, athletes are not "Olympic" just because they compete in the Games or win medals, but rather because they exemplify Olympism. To better understand what this means, we must go beyond our lists of specific examples and look for the abstract quality they all have in common—a personal ideal summarized as "excellence."

Olympism's first Fundamental Principle makes it clear that Olympic excellence is above all an ideal of how people should live their lives:

> Olympism is a philosophy of life, exalting and combining in a balanced whole the qualities of body, will and mind. Blending sport with culture and education, Olympism seeks to create a way of life based on the joy of effort, the educational value of good example, social responsibility and respect for internationally recognised human rights and universal fundamental ethical principles...

The language here is clearly idealistic, and it describes not only a certain kind of person or athlete, but also a certain way of living—an attitude or disposition of character meant to guide the actions of all kinds of people in all kinds of cultures all around the world.

In short, the Olympic ideal of excellence may be understood as the aspiration to improve oneself and one's community every single day and in every single activity. It applies, furthermore, to everyone in the Movement, which is described in the third Fundamental Principle of Olympism as including all those inspired by Olympic ideals. And insofar as the stated goal of the IOC is to promote Olympism, every activity it engages in, from the recruitment of sponsors to the organization of the Games themselves, should aim at encouraging people to adopt this disposition.

The Charter says that "The goal of the Olympic Movement is to contribute to building a peaceful and better world by educating youth through sport practiced in accordance with Olympism and its values." To do this, the Movement must reach well beyond athletes, well beyond youth, and well beyond sport, for that matter. Olympism needs to inspire not just athletic victory, but a certain way of approaching life beyond sport.

Paradox: athletic versus personal excellence

Understanding Olympism as an approach to life creates another paradox. How can athletic excellence, understood in terms of winning competitions or breaking records, inspire a personal ideal of excellence? Obviously, athletic success is what earns athletes a place to compete on an Olympic level, but the personal excellence extolled by Olympism focuses on other qualities not always rewarded by sport.

According to the first Fundamental Principle of Olympism, an example of Olympic excellence would be someone who:

- exalts and combines in a balanced whole the qualities of body, will and mind
- takes joy in effort
- sets a good example
- shows social responsibility
- respects human rights and fundamental ethical principles

These personal virtues may align with the kinds of qualities people admire in Olympic athletes, but strangely, the list says nothing about winning or even sport.

Some might say that athletic success at the elite level actually demands the opposite of these qualities: total dedication to sport, seriousness, selfishness, pushing the limits of the rules, caring only for victory and nothing else. Perhaps those are extremes embodied by few, if any, successful athletes, but it is clear that elite sport today does not reliably reward the moral dispositions extolled by Olympism. Aside from special recognition for heroic acts of fair play, such as the Pierre de Coubertin medal, athletes are rewarded for their competitive performances. The Olympic

Games may create an atmosphere that encourages and even celebrates the display of dispositions that align with its personal ideal, but few athletes reach the Olympic level by prioritizing human rights and social responsibility. In short, the realities of modern sport can make it difficult for Olympic athletes to live the kind of life and have the kind of virtues they are supposed to exemplify.

This paradox is partially resolved by noting that Olympic athletes function primarily as symbols of the ideal of excellence to be promoted. But reality matters as much as ideas do, and if we believe that balancing body, will, and mind means that a person should at least have the liberty to preserve their mental and physical health, pursue their education, and maintain a stable personal life, we may notice a glaring conflict between the personal (and moral) excellence lauded by Olympism and the athletic excellence rewarded in the Olympic Games.

What is more, the pursuit of athletic success places pressure on athletes, sometimes in a way that jeopardizes their physical, mental, and personal well-being. Neglecting the well-being of the very people you set up as examples of an ideal is, as professor of public health Verner Møller has noted, bald-faced hypocrisy. The educational value of Olympic ideals is diminished when the reality of sport is allowed to drift away from them. Indeed, the conflict may cause us to wonder where the link between athletic performance and personal excellence came from.

Ancient Greek *aretē*

The answer, unsurprisingly, is ancient Greece, which had a concept of personal excellence called *aretē* that was closely linked to athletics. In fact, the very concept of an "athlete" can be traced to heroes like Heracles, whose amazing feats or "labors" were called *athloi.* Heroes served as models of *aretē* in ancient Greek culture, and it is no coincidence that sculptures featuring Heracles's *athloi* decorated the Temple of Zeus in Olympia (and are visible in its museum today).

The religious context of ancient athletics is based on the contrast between the perfection of gods, the imperfection humans, and the excellence of heroes, whose *athloi* bring them closer to divinity. The contests have roots in hero worship, which sought to awaken a hero's life-giving spirit. The athletes' efforts to emulate the *athloi* of heroes in sport effectively brings their excellence to life. It seems plausible, in this religious context, that spectators witnessing a superb athletic performance at the Olympic

Games might have experienced it as an epiphany—the brief appearance of a god or divine hero.

It is reasonable to say that mythological stories of heroic *athloi* exhibit the features of personal excellence described in the Fundamental Principles of Olympism. For example, the story of Heracles's first labor, slaying the Nemean lion, recounts how it challenged his body, his will, and his mind. Since the animal's hide was impervious to arrows, he first figured out how to trap it in a cave, then he bravely grabbed hold of it and suffocated it with his enormous strength. The feat also exhibited social responsibility because the animal had been terrorizing locals and killing their livestock. Heroic *athloi* were used to educate by example through the myriad songs and stories that celebrated them and the athletic contests that emulated them.

Though athletic *aretē* is merely a replica of heroic *aretē*, training for it came to be understood as a form of moral education—a process of making oneself more like a hero or god. Heracles's labors are also called *ponoi*, the plural of *ponos* (effort), which came to be seen, with the help of philosophers like Plato, as the true path to *aretē*. Previously, *aretē* had been considered a matter of birth and heredity, so the idea that it could be trained had special appeal for marginalized people, such as those disqualified from citizenship because they didn't have the right bloodlines. In Athens, these outcasts gathered at the gymnasium dedicated to Heracles and tried to achieve *aretē* through *ponos,* like he had.

So, Olympism's link between athletic and personal excellence finds its roots in the ancient ideal of *aretē,* understood as striving to become as much like a god or hero as you can (or, in modern terms, to become the best version of yourself) by engaging in joyful effort. An "athlete" in this context is anyone who makes a serious effort to pursue personal excellence—whether they compete in sport or not.

Modern Olympic excellence

The modern Olympic value of excellence, as illustrated in the First Fundamental Principle of Olympism encourages "a way of life based on the joy of effort." This echoes the ancient Greek connection between *ponos* and *aretē,* which linked social worth with virtue and achievement rather than class or wealth. In a similar way, Coubertin saw the effort-based achievements of egalitarian sport as capable of establishing an alternative, merit-based aristocracy (despite his membership in the traditional aristocracy).

For Coubertin, athletes in the "springtime" of human life represented this new personal ideal, not least because they had freed their bodies from "the tyranny of dissolute passions" through sport (1935). The joy of effort displayed by athletes in competition was thought to offer an idealized vision of humanity imbued with educational power and capable of inspiring even the unathletic masses toward self-improvement.

Accordingly, Coubertin emphasized the significance of effort, stating that Olympic pedagogy is based on a "cult of effort" (1918) and praising sport as a venue where we can observe "effort opposing effort for the love of effort itself" (1935). Indeed, he sought to replace the growing perception of sport as a battlefield where athletes perform a "struggle for survival" with a vision of education that interprets effort as a "struggle for success," not limited to sport but capable of extending to all human activities (1913).

Hans Lenk, philosophy professor and Olympic gold medalist in rowing at the 1960 Games, recognized that Coubertin's advocacy for effort in any endeavor of life had strong pedagogical foundations since, philosophically speaking, the individual striving to achieve excellence represents a powerful symbol—an expression of humanity's eternal orientation toward the better.

The Olympic Games, from this perspective, are not primarily concerned with identifying the best athletes in the world but rather with celebrating their efforts toward excellence as a means of inspiring meaningful lives beyond sport. As former president of the International Olympic Academy, Nikolaos Nissiotis explains, Olympism is

> a means for educating the whole man as a conscious citizen of the world [...] through adherence to ethical principles valid in universal dimensions.

Olympism envisions a never-ending educational project that aims to revive the ancient Greek ideal of *aretē* in its modern form of personal excellence as expressed by Coubertin. The ideal venue for promoting this personal ideal is the Olympic Games, in which athletes become inspiring symbols of excellence by embodying the goals of Olympism through their actions both in and beyond sport.

How sport evokes and inspires excellence

Superficially, it is not difficult to see how the practice of sport evokes excellence. Some philosophers even define sports in terms of effort and excellence, for example, Bernard Suits's "voluntary effort to overcome unnecessary obstacles," and Simon's "quest for excellence through challenge." These analyses illustrate how sport contrives artificial difficulties that demand personal virtues in order to be overcome. To perform well athletically, you are called upon to harmonize body, will, and mind; engage enthusiastically in the effort of training; respect the rules of the game and the people who make it possible.

In other words, athletic performance tends to call forth the qualities extolled in the first Fundamental Principle of Olympism. These aspects of an athlete's performance are under their control, part of their personal agency, in contrast with things outside their control, such as genetic traits, access to good nutrition, coaching, and equipment. In celebrating Olympic athletes, however, we specifically celebrate the excellence that derives from their personal agency because this is the disposition that drives achievement beyond sport. Those who win without trying hard do not fulfill the Olympic ideal.

Just as Heracles' path to *aretē* required *ponoi,* Olympic excellence requires participants not just to progress, but to do so by means of personal effort. The Olympic athlete knows that she needs to spend endless hours training, refining technique, analyzing mistakes, and enduring pain, exhaustion, and frustration. Indeed, effort is what athletes share with achievers in every field. In academia, for instance, researchers know that to achieve excellence, they need to spend hours reading, struggling with ideas, debating with peers, facing confusion and frustration, and enduring the tough writing process.

Excellence, however, is never an end state; both the academic and the athlete know that the qualities that enabled their best possible performance must be constantly exercised in order to be retained. Excellence is a moral disposition expressed in the never-ending process of striving to improve through effort. What we celebrate in the Olympic Games is not so much the athlete's individual success but the personal excellence that their efforts exemplify.

Sport evokes excellence by challenging athletes, and it inspires excellence in others by motivating the general moral disposition of self-improvement. This might conjure the debate over whether athletes should be role models, but the reality is that they are, whether they should be or not, and whether they choose to be or not. In fact, we all are. As the French philosopher Jean-Paul Sartre once observed, in choosing for ourselves, we choose for all mankind. This is because our public actions make a statement about what we think the right thing to do is, and we cannot "opt out" of responsibility for that.

An Olympic athlete is no *more* responsible for the example they set than any other person in the world, but the example they set, especially in the Games, typically has *more impact* than others. Athletes are *not* role models in the sense that they should inspire others to play the "role" of elite athlete—as we know, that role is achievable for very few. Rather, like the ancient Greek model in which heroes serve as models of *aretē* to be emulated in athletics, Olympic athletes act as "character models" who serve the Movement by embodying and encouraging its ideals.

The motto versus the creed

A deeper understanding of Olympism's ideal of personal excellence can help us to reconcile the apparent conflict between the Olympic motto:

> *Citius, Altius, Fortius - Communiter*
> (Faster, Higher, Stronger – Together)

and the traditional Olympic creed, which was inspired by Bishop Ethelbert Talbot and embraced by Coubertin:

> The important thing in life is not the triumph, but the fight; the essential thing is not to have won, but to have fought well.

The motto privileges athletic performance, while the creed emphasizes participation. But, as philosopher Cesar Torres has noted, the two aren't really in conflict because participation in sport is necessary to achieve athletic success, and since the objective of every Olympic contest, as defined by its rules, is victory, participants need to struggle or, as the creed puts it, fight, in order to "play the game."

In fact, the value of victory and of athletic success itself depends on this idea of effort and struggle, that is, on the personal excellence that underpins it. Winning the lottery or any game of chance does not demand effort and struggle, and therefore cannot be a symbol of personal excellence. If we admire lottery winners, it is not for the excellence that led to their victory. At the same time, we may celebrate someone who embodies the Olympic motto not by racing faster, jumping higher, or being stronger than a competitor, but by being faster, higher, and stronger than they were before.

It is easy to see how this athletic attitude aligns with the moral disposition of Olympic excellence, understood as striving for personal improvement. It is exemplified by the Olympic Games' inclusion of "solidarity" athletes exempted from qualifying standards to achieve national diversity, most of whom are not medal contenders but often set personal and national records because of the Olympic atmosphere.

Returning to Olympism's ideal of personal excellence, we can now see how a concept like the "joy of effort" reconciles the motto and creed. As Coubertin said in 1901,

> The sportsman remains a stranger to utilitarian concerns. The task that he accomplishes is one that he has set for himself. Since he does not need to return to his task the very next day to earn his living, there is no reason for him to conserve his energy. In this way he is able to cultivate effort for effort's sake, to seek out obstacles, to place a few obstacles in his own path, and always to aim a little higher than the level he must achieve. It is this idea that is so well expressed by the motto chosen by Fr. Didon for his students at Arcueil, who had formed an athletic association. At their first meeting, he told them, 'Here is your watchword: *citius, altius, fortius*! Faster, higher, stronger!'

The essence of Olympism's personal ideal of excellence is voluntary engagement in struggle for the sake of improving oneself and setting an example for others. Understanding the value of that struggle creates joy, whether victory is achieved or not, and whether the struggle is athletic or not.

Critics and challenges

Olympism's faith in the "educational value of good example" is frequently challenged by critics who point to the countless cases of athletes seeking victory through means other than effort, such as doping or by exploiting legal advantages like high-tech equipment unavailable to opponents. Such behaviors undermine the personal agency that gives victory its moral value, diminishing the personal excellence extolled in Olympism.

Scholars trace the problem to a mentality that understands success quantitatively in terms of records and medals. The Olympic Motto has been said to encourage this mindset, which in turn fosters excessive specialization—a tendency that historian Allen Guttmann described as "the beginning of evil" in sport. According to psychologist Daniel Gould, specialization in sport brings undesirable psychological effects such as emotional stress, burnout, and loss of motivation. Philosopher Sigmund Loland also links it with morally problematic actions like doping. Indeed, it is easy to observe that for most elite-level athletes today, medals and records are more of a priority than the Olympic ideal of personal excellence.

Athletes themselves are not the source of this mentality, however. Sociologists like Richard Gruneau argue that it arises from the social structuration of sport that occurs within institutions. This process establishes and legitimizes assumptions, values, and beliefs about sport, which become resistant to change. Scholars Cecilia Stenling and Josef Fahlén have demonstrated that the dominant institutional approaches to sport center on results and commerce—orientations that reinforce one another since victories attract sponsors and generate profit. The moral and educational well-being of the athlete seems to be valued only insofar as it serves these institutional priorities.

This anti-Olympic approach is reinforced in many universities, where sports science programs focus on performance while management programs treat sport merely as a source of profit. Indeed, it is not difficult to observe that institutions under the Olympic umbrella, including National Olympic Committees (NOCs) and International Sports Federations (IFs), tend to measure their success in terms of medals and revenue. As long as Olympic institutions understand excellence merely as a means to money and medals, it is hard to expect athletes to think of it Olympically.

The Olympic Charter makes it clear that the goal of organizations within the Movement is "to promote the fundamental principles and values of Olympism." If they focus instead on medals and sponsorship, they violate that obligation. The Movement could abandon all pretense of its philosophical goals and simply embrace the business of sport without regard to the moral dispositions associated with it, but as anthropologist Sören Damkjaer argues, the very idea of Olympism risks becoming meaningless if it loses its ethical foundation.

In other words, the Olympic ideal of excellence that is symbolized by athletes begins within organizations, which have a responsibility to resist the anti-Olympic conventions that prevail in modern sport. Rather than encouraging athletes to engage in sport for the sake of records and medals, NOCs should better support their ability to train in a healthy, supportive environment aligned with Olympic ideals. Instead of investing in performance-enhancing technologies, Olympic organizations should invest in athletes by optimizing their agency and well-being. Some athletes feel like they have to sacrifice personal excellence for the sake of athletic results; the mission of Olympic institutions should be to make sport serve the ideal of excellence and not the other way around.

Conclusion

Olympic athletes exemplify the personal dimension of Olympism, namely an approach to life that aims at constant self-improvement in any activity. Athletic success is linked with but not identical to personal excellence; in fact, elite sport is not usually associated with the qualities extolled in the Fundamental Principles of Olympism. But Olympic Sport can be managed in a way that preserves the link between personal and athletic excellence, not just at a personal level but at an institutional level as well.

Olympism celebrates the *ideal* of excellence, not the excellence of any single person. That may sound insensitive, but actually, it is liberating for athletes and admirers alike. No one can win every event, and no one is perfect, but if we understand the Olympic ideal as a commitment to pursuing excellence, it doesn't really matter if the athlete loses, or even confesses that they hate training. The athlete merely symbolizes the ideal that Olympism really celebrates, and insofar as the Olympic Movement is a group of people inspired by these ideals, Olympic excellence begins with us in everything we do.

Questions for reflection and discussion

1. In your own professional context (coaching, teaching, managing), what challenges make it difficult to cultivate or uphold the kind of excellence demanded by Olympism?
2. Identify some specific ways that Olympic organizations promote personal excellence beyond athletic performance. How might they do even better?

References

Coubertin, P. (1901). Sports Psychology. In N. Müller ed. 2000 (pp. 141-148).

Coubertin, P. (1913). Olympisme et Utilitarisme. *Revue Olympique*. No.89. (pp. 68-73).

Coubertin, P. (1918). Olympic Letter V: Olympic Pedagogy. In N. Müller ed. 2000 (pp. 555-59).

Coubertin, P. (1935). The Fundamentals of the Philosophy of the Modern Olympics. *Olympic Review* 56 (1956): 52-54.

Damkjaer, S. (2004). Post-Olympism and the Aestheticization of Sport. In J. Bale & M. Christensen (Eds.), *Post Olympism? Questioning Sport in the Twenty-first Century* (pp. 211-230). Berg.

Gruneau, R. (1983). *Class, Sport and Social Development*. University of Massachusetts Press.

Gould, D. (2010). Early sport specialization: A psychological perspective. *Journal of Physical Education, Recreation & Dance, 81*(8), 33-37.

Guttmann, A. (1978). *From Ritual to Record: The nature of modern sports*. Columbia University Press.

Lenk, H. (2007). An anthropology of the Olympic athlete: towards a modernized philosophy of the Olympic Games and athletes. *Journal of Olympic History*, 15(1), 39-47.

Loland, S. (2004). The Vulnerability Thesis and its Consequences: a Critique of Specialization in Olympic Sport. In J. Bale & M. Christensen (Eds.), *Post-Olympism: Questioning Sport in the Twenty-first Century* (pp. 189-199). Berg.

Møller, V. (2004). Doping and the Olympic Games from an aesthetic perspective. In J. Bale & M. Christensen (Eds.), *Post-Olympism: Questioning Sport in the Twenty-first Century* (pp. 201-210). Berg.

Nissiotis, N. (1984). Olympism and Today's Reality. In *International Olympic Academy Twenty-Fourth Session* (pp. 57-74). IOC.

Simon, R. L. (2014). Theories of sport. In Cesar R. Torres, *The Bloomsbury Companion to the Philosophy of Sport* (pp. 83-97). Bloomsbury.

Stenling, C., & Fahlén, J. (2009). The order of logics in Swedish sport–feeding the hungry beast of result orientation and commercialization. *European journal for sport and society, 6*(2), 121-134.

Suits, B. (1978). *The Grasshopper: Games, Life and Utopia.* University of Toronto Press.

Torres, C. (2006). Results or Participation? Reconsidering Olympism's Approach to Competition. *Quest 58*(2), 242-54.

III

What Makes Olympic Sport Special?

The interpersonal ideal of Respect

As in the case of athletes, there is something special about Olympic sport that distinguishes it from the same activities played under the same rules outside of the Games. In other words, it is not the sport itself that is different, it is the attitude with which people approach it that is special. According to the fourth Fundamental Principle of Olympism, what is special about Olympic sport is that it is practiced in the "Olympic Spirit":

> The practice of sport is a human right. Every individual must have access to the practice of sport, without discrimination of any kind in respect of internationally recognised human rights within the remit

> of the Olympic Movement. The Olympic spirit requires mutual understanding with a spirit of friendship, solidarity and fair play.

We can all recall moments in the Olympic Games when the Olympic spirit is expressed by athletes shaking hands or helping opponents. The moral dispositions associated with that spirit can be summarized as an interpersonal ideal of respect. It is no coincidence that the IOC website states that the Olympic value of respect stems from an effort "to preserve human dignity."

Respect for human rights and ethical principles is also part of the personal ideal described in Olympism's first Fundamental Principle, but the fourth principle, quoted above, focuses on how we should ideally treat one another, namely, with an attitude that everyone belongs and everyone matters. It also declares that the practice of sport is a human right—a valuable activity shared collectively on the basis of our common humanity. This implies not only a responsibility to reduce barriers to participation and other forms of discrimination; it also demands that we share the universal human good of sport with a certain kind of "spirit."

The moral disposition of "friendship, solidarity and fair play" is supposed to characterize not only how athletes should treat one another within competition, but how individuals should treat each other in society—whether they are competing or not. As we said before, this is an *ideal* of how people should interact, not always the reality of how they actually do. Currently, sport is not listed in the Universal Declaration of Human Rights, and rarely is it practiced "without discrimination of any kind," as Olympism demands.

If you ask people to list moments in sports history that are characteristically Olympic, however, they will often point to interactions in which athletes display just these kinds of respectful attitudes—for example, the way the German athlete Luz Long helped African-American Jesse Owens to qualify for the long jump at the 1936 Berlin Games, in spite of Hitler's racist ideology. Of course, we cannot know if Long and Owens really felt the Olympic spirit at the Games, but their story serves as an expression of the respect that Olympism proposes as an ideal of how people should treat one another.

Furthermore, like the personal ideal of excellence exemplified by the athlete, this interpersonal ideal of respect is supposed to be part of Olympism's philosophy of life; in other words, it should govern all of our interpersonal interactions, not just those within sport. At the same time, the very nature of sport provides a foundation for this ideal of respect, and it is primarily through watching and participating in sport that we are expected to develop it as a moral disposition.

Paradox: conflict and competition

The interpersonal ideal exemplified by sport raises another paradox: how can competition foster respect when its goal is to dominate the opponent? Even when the rules are respected, sports can seem like forms of conflict in which two or more sides strive for the incompatible outcome of victory. George Orwell famously described sports as "war minus the shooting" because he thought they inspired attitudes among competitors typical of enemies at war. Yet Olympism expects competition to promote moral dispositions like mutual understanding, friendship, solidarity, and fair play.

How can wrestling teach non-discrimination when it is designed to distinguish winners from losers? How does striking your opponent in boxing or Taekwondo cultivate mutual understanding? How can willful deception of opponents with everything from head-fakes to game-plans count as solidarity? These kinds of actions would not be considered respectful, much less fair in practices like law or business, so how can an activity that encourages and even rewards them foster the kind of respect aligned with the Olympic spirit?

Like other paradoxes, this one can be resolved by a deeper understanding of sport. Unlike some other forms of conflict, especially war, athletic competition demands not just respect for the rules but also for opponents. Competitors in any sport not only make the contest itself possible, but they also provide the challenge needed to cultivate personal excellence; in other words, competitors benefit one another. The temporary conflict embedded in sport serves the larger goal of improvement through competition—a term that derives from the Latin verb *com-petere* (to strive together)

It doesn't matter if we dislike our opponents or disagree with their personal life-choices; sport demands that we respect them and their role in the contest. In this way, sport teaches us to respect other people *despite* any conflict we may have with them; to set aside personal differences so that productive competition can take place. And as we experience the basic respect for others demanded by sport, whether as participants or as spectators, our ability to overcome social prejudices and interact fairly with people beyond sport increases—especially when the competition is experienced in an atmosphere imbued with the "Olympic spirit."

The Olympic ideal of respect is a moral disposition that builds upon the foundational respect demanded by sport, and it extends beyond sport to govern all of our interactions with others. It consists not only in following (i.e., respecting) the rules of the relevant activity (whatever that may be), but also in adopting an attitude towards others that cannot be imposed by rules or enforced by officials. This attitude derives from a deeper understanding of competition—not just in sports, but in life—as something more than zero-sum conflict that only benefits the winner. It recognizes not only the nature of sport, but the value of those who make the shared activity possible.

Indeed, the word *respect* comes from the Latin *respectare,* which literally means "to look back at someone." In this sense, Olympic respect seeks to recover that original meaning; it is not an act of obedience or politeness, but rather one that looks at others with regard, consideration, and attention—the attitude that everyone belongs and everyone matters.

Ancient Greek *aidōs*

It is puzzling that the roots of Olympic respect reach back to the Ancient Greeks, since their societies were hardly paragons of inclusion and equality. Wide differences of nobility and economic class were compounded by hostility among different ethnic and political groupings. War and enmity were commonplace, and sport was only made possible by an agreement to set aside hostilities for the sake of religious worship. The Olympic Games provided a sanctuary from social norms by treating competitors as equals—an ideal symbolized by their nudity, which all but eliminated signs of ethnic and class difference while invoking *aidōs,* an emotion that combines shame and respect for others.

In ancient Greek religion, the naked human form also reflected the image of the gods and heroes that athletes sought to emulate and celebrate. At Olympia, humans presented an ideal version of themselves to the gods in an atmosphere of reverence (another translation for *aidōs*). Disrespecting the contest by bribery or other forms of cheating was a religious offense punished by fines used to set up statues of Zeus by the stadium entrance that deterred others with inscriptions like "the contest at Olympia is one of *aretē* and not of wealth" (Pausanias 5.21.7).

The confusion of merit with wealth and social status is common even today, but the religious goals of sport at Olympia seem to have inspired reflection about and changes to interpersonal attitudes in ancient Greek society. According to Philostratus, the first athletic event at Olympia was a footrace to the altar to determine who would have the honor of lighting the sacrificial flame—an honor that, in sacrificial logic, needs to go to the "best" among those present. Normally, a tribe would just designate its king, but since many tribes were present at Olympia, the selection must have posed a problem. It is plausible that, out of reverence for the preferences of the god, worshippers set up the impartial and publicly visible mechanism of a footrace to discover who was most worthy.

Social bias still motivated the exclusion of women, foreigners, and slaves from the Games. When a Spartan princess won anyway by taking advantage of a loophole that awards Olympic crowns to the horses' owners in equestrian events, critics called it proof that victory was the result of wealth rather than *aretē* (Plutarch 20.1). Aristocrats are said to have avoided direct competition with athletes of lower birth (Isocrates 16.33), and there was apparently an attempt to exclude Alexander I of Macedon from an Olympic footrace on the basis of him being a "foreigner" (Herodotus 5.22.2).

Ancient Olympic sport, like its modern counterpart, was not immune from the social prejudices that undermine respect and fairness, but the religious atmosphere mitigated those forces. Sport arguably provided a model of fairness that was meaningfully different from the "might makes right" principle common in Greek society (though rejected in Plato's *Republic*).

It should not be forgotten that ancient Greece is also the home of democracy, which, as archaeologist Stephen Miller points out, shares principles with sport such as equality before the law and the opportunity to participate (at least in theory). These privileges were limited to free-born Greek males in sport and politics alike, but the equality of opportunity and reward according to merit showcased by sport plausibly contributed to the democratic ideals for which ancient Greece is celebrated. The *aidōs* demanded by the ancient Olympic Games generated a logic of fair play and inclusion that inspired interpersonal respect.

Modern Olympic Respect

The modern Olympic revivalists understood that their global aims could not be attached to any particular religion, but they tried to retain the ancient atmosphere of respect by imagining athletic ideals themselves as a kind of religion. Coubertin's notion of *religio athletae* does not replace conventional religion, but celebrates humanity. It signals an understanding of and reverence for sport that draws one toward recognizing and caring for others within the competition and beyond. Philosopher Ivo Jirásek describes *religio athletae* as "a religious attitude that is based on mutual respect and overcomes confessional differences."

The cultivation of mutual respect had always been a guiding value in Coubertin's educational project, as philosopher Lisa Reithmann notes, because he saw it as a requirement for societies to function properly. It was so important, in fact, that Coubertin devoted an entire book to it in 1915—*Le Respect Mutuel*—published as part of the final volume of his trilogy, *The Education of Adolescents in the XXth Century*.

Coubertin argued that the ideal combines respect for beliefs, conditions, conventions, and individuality. The first form recognizes that humans are guided by different convictions, which give direction and meaning to their lives and therefore must be respected. The second acknowledges that people occupy different social positions, but insists that they stand on the same moral level and should never be treated differently based on their social condition. The third pertains to laws and customs that structure social practices, which deserve respect—despite being imperfect—for the sake of collective progress. Finally, respect for individuality refers to the diversity of personalities and life choices. Whether one chooses to become an artist, professor, or farmer, to marry or remain single, to leave a job or stay in the same career for life—such personal decisions must likewise be respected even when they diverge from our own. Although sport is not the main focus in *Le Respect Mutuel,* it is not difficult to see how Coubertin imagined that the Olympic project could serve the ideal.

Coubertin understood that respect was cultivated by creating a "culture of conscience" in which individuals remain aware and acknowledge differences. He believed this culture could be nurtured through sport, which he called an "indirect stimulus for ethics" (1910). In sports, individuals abide by the same rules and conventions, thereby respecting a "common good," shared with diverse others. In a time of great division among the social classes, Coubertin (1913) observed that sport could place people on equal footing, not in terms of "resources," but of "manners," thereby creating egalitarian relationships that invite participants to get to know one another. He observed that sport reduces "social distance, at times eliminating it altogether, and at times going so far as to overturn the social hourglass by placing a humble craftsman higher than a prince" (1913).

Yet, to make sport a direct stimulus for ethics, Coubertin maintained that "we must make the purpose of sport the creation of a sense of solidarity, which will cause sport to reach beyond itself" (1910). For Coubertin, the Olympic spirit provides an atmosphere that enables sport to create "brothers in arms" able to foster bonds "stronger than that of mere camaraderie" (1935).

How sport evokes and inspires respect

Coubertin observed that the feelings of reverence which underpin mutual respect were often present in athletic competitions, but to make this sentiment flourish, athletes would have to preserve the spirit of competition and fair play at the center of his *religio athletae*. What, precisely, does "the spirit of competition and fair play" mean?

Gaffney argues that athletic competitions are morally important places where people learn to recognize one another. This moral recognition begins when participants acknowledge their opponent as someone who shares the same desire to compete. This generates a sense of reciprocity, collaboration, and interdependency. Then, in a second moment of recognition, each competitor not only agrees to act within the rules that define the activity but also depends on the other to do the same, thereby creating an environment of commitment, trust, and loyalty. In this sense, athletic competitions are not just interpersonal activities, but they depend on competitors mutually recognizing one another; indeed, athletic skills only gain meaning through the presence of others.

Similarly, philosopher Drew Hyland argues that athletic competitions are ethically significant because competitors improve each other through mutual striving—a mark of friendship—and also because contests require us to give our full attention to others. In sports, we are fully absorbed, active, and dedicated to others while trying to complete the task. Psychologist Mihály Csikszentmihalyi adds that when we immerse ourselves completely in an activity demanding effort and attention, we enter the *flow experience* where "we lose a sense of ourselves" in the action. But if, in sports, our actions gain meaning only through others, then we also lose a sense of ourselves in others.

Within competition, athletes are fully engaged with the movements, tactics, and skills of their opponents. They cannot be indifferent to each other; indeed, each deserves care and regard, since they constitute the limits and possibilities of the activity. Sports direct our attention toward others, pushing us away from selfishness and individualism. In a way, the spirit of competition dissolves the divide between rivals, for although in opposition, they form a shared and cooperative "we" because the activity itself depends on their mutual engagement.

The value of competition as moral education cannot be realized without fair play (an essential element of the Olympic spirit). Fair play functions as the "glue" that holds the spirit of competition together because it ensures that opponents remain faithful to the competitive relationship imposed by the game. Philosophers Robert Butcher and Angela Schneider frame fair play philosophically as "respect for the game," an attitude that goes beyond respecting the rules and implies a commitment to the integrity of the activity itself.

This means that athletes sometimes act in ways not required by the written rules in order to preserve the spirit of competition. In football, for example, it includes kicking the ball out so an injured player can get medical attention; in cross-country skiing, coaches may hand a replacement pole to an opposing racer who has broken hers. Such actions not only ensure that contests are decided by the athletic skills they were designed to test, but also that the competitors continue to relate to one another through an interpersonal ideal of respect.

The Olympic Oath

The Olympic Movement has never been immune to forces that corrupt its interpersonal ideal of respect. Coubertin wrote as early as 1908 that the Olympic idea was under threat because attitudes of fair play were being replaced by the increasing "madness of gaming," which engendered a "lamentable atmosphere of jealousy, envy, vanity, and mistrust." Indeed, he remarked that when participants fail to uphold fair play, it reveals a "state of mind that prevail[s]" among them.

Today, this concern is called the "win-at-all-costs" mentality—an attitude that brings selfish sentiments into the competitive arena, and is expressed in disrespectful practices such as doping, cheating, bribery, and even violence. Such corruptive forces threaten sport's ability to educate positive moral dispositions like respect because they erode the loyalty and generosity at the heart of Coubertin's *religio athletae.*

In order to shore up that potential, Coubertin insisted that athletes take an oath, like they had in ancient times, to compete for the glory of sport and not their own interests. "We must get back to something similar," he said in 1906, otherwise "we will see the beginnings of decline in our modern sport, a decline that will become faster and faster." The modern Olympic Oath was introduced at the 1920 Antwerp Games (after the 1916 Games were cancelled due to World War I), and continues to be taken today in the name of judges, coaches, and officials. The modern Oath expresses well the Olympic ideal of respect:

> We promise to take part in these Olympic Games, respecting and abiding by the rules and in the spirit of fair play, inclusion and equality. Together we stand in solidarity and commit ourselves to sport without doping, without cheating, without any form of discrimination. We do this for the honor of our teams, in respect for the Fundamental Principles of Olympism, and to make the world a better place through sport.

Notably, the promise applies both to the rules of sport and the Olympic spirit, evoking the idea of an honor-based community driven by commitments to fairness and integrity. The Oath, said Coubertin in 1906, "will introduce into modern sport the spirit of joyful candor, the spirit of sincere altruism that will renew them, and will make of collective muscular exercise a true school for moral improvement."

The Oath locates the motivation for this respect in Olympism and in the pursuit of mutual improvement, symbolizing the aspiration to build human relationships grounded in Olympic ideals and regard for others—making a better and peaceful world through sport. In abiding by the Oath, participants resist the social and economic forces that diminish fair play, and ensure that their interactions with others are grounded in respect—not only in sport but also in the greater game of life.

Critics and challenges

Despite their promise to abide by the Olympic Oath, critics argue that athletes routinely act against the Olympic spirit, particularly fair play. Orwell even claimed that the sporting spirit "has nothing to do with fair play," a view accepted by Damkjaer, who observed that repeated violations of fair play at the Olympic Games reveal the "demoralization of ideals" in modern sport.

The IOC has taken measures to safeguard the Olympic ideals. At the London 2012 Games, for instance, badminton players intentionally tried to lose their matches to secure a more favorable playoff draw—an incident that shows how a victory-only mindset can erode fair play and diminish effort without violating the rules. They were ultimately disqualified for failing to use their "best efforts to win" and for behaving in a manner detrimental to sport. Their actions failed to honor the value of effort and the goal of the competitive relationship.

The same can be said of conventions like trash-talking, professional fouls, or time-wasting, which, though accepted in some sporting cultures, erode the integrity of the contest. Such behaviors reveal selfish attitudes focused solely on securing an advantage rather than seeking mutual improvement —in short, a lack of respect.

Fair play also has an institutional dimension, and critics note that Olympic organizations themselves frequently fall short of it. They argue that fair play must be upheld not only in words but also in actions, for example, by taking into account material conditions that tilt the level playing field. In today's Olympic Games, wealth inequalities continue to shape access to and outcomes in competition. These disparities are manifest in unequal access to sport technology and equipment, training facilities, coaching, and medical support. It is no coincidence that Olympic podiums are mostly occupied by athletes from wealthy countries.

As sociologist Pierre Bourdieu put it, "those who talk of equality of opportunity forget that social games [...] are not 'fair'." This standpoint, reveals that institutions have an expanded responsibility to uphold the Oath in terms of ensuring equality of opportunity. Since it seems impossible to eliminate all such social disparities, however, scholars like Ramón Spaaij say that sport cannot help but reinforce social divisions and marginalization.

Recognizing such shortcomings does not negate sport's power to cultivate respect; rather, it invites reflection on how that power might be improved. On the field of play, for example, many athletes salute, shake hands, or bow to one another—gestures that symbolize respect. Athletes and institutions can also actively resist the "win-at-all-costs" mentality with acts of "fair play" like helping fallen competitors or assisting with broken equipment. An attitude of respect is even shown among spectators who stand respectfully when the winner's national anthem is played. For philosopher Kenneth Aggerholm, such gestures count as "moral acts" that express the commitment to sport and to others embodied in the ideal of respect.

At the institutional level, respect can be cultivated through policies that address the wealth inequalities embedded in the Olympic system. In equestrian competitions at the Youth Olympic Games (YOG), for example, horses are provided to participants through a random draw, ensuring a fairer contest by reducing the influence of economic disparities. Similar measures could be replicated in other sports, helping ensure that athletes compete under comparable material conditions. Olympic sport evokes and inspires respect by fostering fair play in competition and within institutions.

Conclusion

Olympic sport is special because it embodies an interpersonal ideal of respect demonstrated in a moral disposition that expresses the idea that everyone belongs and everyone matters. This attitude derives from an understanding of competition that reaches beyond the goal of victory and appreciates the other people who make the social benefits of sport possible. The Olympic Spirit is a collective ethos that cannot be legislated either in sport or the world at large; it involves escalating levels of respect: from basic non-discrimination, to friendship, solidarity, fair-play, and ultimately social justice. This last ideal may be called political when it involves large groups of people, especially nations—as we will discuss in the next chapter.

Questions for reflection and discussion

1. Much of sport focuses on enforcing rules, yet Olympic respect is deeper than rule-following. How can sports institutions (clubs, NOCs) cultivate a culture of respect that goes beyond mere compliance with rules?

2. Recount a favorite moment in Olympic sport that expresses the ideal of respect. Is there anything that can be done to encourage and promote such moments?

References

Aggerholm, K. (2025). Sport humanism: Contours of a humanist theory of sport. *Journal of the Philosophy of Sport, 52*(1), 1-24.

Bourdieu, P. (2000). *Pascalian Meditations*. Stanford University Press.

Butcher, R., & Schneider, A. (1998). Fair play as respect for the game. *Journal of the Philosophy of Sport, 25*(1), 1-22.

Coubertin, P. (1906). The Athletes' Oath (Letter to Charles Simon). In N. Müller ed. 2000 (pp. 598-599).

Coubertin, P. (1908). The Trustees of the Olympic Idea. In N. Müller ed. 2000 (pp. 587-589).

Coubertin, P. (1908). Why I Revived the Olympic Games. In N. Müller ed. 2000 (pp. 542-546).

Coubertin, P. (1908). The Fourth Olympiad (London 1908). In N. Müller ed. 2000 (pp. 420-425).

Coubertin, P. (1910). Sports and Ethics. In Müller ed. 2000 (pp. 167-169).

Coubertin, P. (1913). Sport and the Social Issue. In N. Müller ed. 2000 (pp. 214-216).

Coubertin, P. (1915). Le Respect Mutuel. *L'éducation des adolescents au XXe siècle*. III Education Morale. Alcan.

Coubertin, P. (1935). The Fundamentals of the Philosophy of the Modern Olympics. *Olympic Review* 56 (1956), 52-54.

Csikszentmihalyi, M. (1991). *Flow: The Psychology of Optimal Experience.* Harper.

Damkjaer, S. (2004). Post-Olympism and the Aestheticization of Sport. In J. Bale & M. Christensen (Eds.), *Post Olympism? Questioning Sport in the Twenty-first Century* (pp. 211-230). Berg.

Gaffney, P. (2015) Competition. In M. McNamee & W.J. Morgan (Eds.), *Routledge Handbook of the Philosophy of Sport* (pp. 287-299). Routledge.

Hyland, D. (1977). "And That Is The Best Part of Us:" Human Beings and Play. *Journal of the Philosophy of Sport*, 4(1), 36-49.

International Olympic Committee (n.d). *Olympic values – excellence, respect, and friendship.* https://www.olympics.com/ioc/olympic-values

Jirásek, I. (2015). Religion, Spirituality, and Sport: From *Religio Athletae* Toward *Spiritus Athletae. Quest, 67*(3), 290–299.

Miller, S.G. (2004). *Ancient Greek Athletics.* Yale University Press.

Orwell, G. (1945). The Sporting Spirit. *Tribune 468*(14), 10-11.

Spaaij, R., Magee, J., & Jeanes, R. (2014). *Sport and Social Exclusion in Global Society*. Routledge.

Reithmann, L. (2010). Coubertin's idea of 'mutual respect' according to Kant's concept of moral philosophy. In *Proceedings: International Symposium for Olympic Research* (pp. 44-51). International Centre for Olympic Studies.

IV

What Makes the Olympic Rings Special?

The community ideal of friendship

Olympism also posits a community ideal which can be described as (international) friendship. This diverges from the ordinary understanding of friendship as affection between individuals, focusing instead on nations since the modern Olympic Movement has a global vision. As explained in the third Fundamental Principle of Olympism:

> The Olympic Movement is the concerted, organised, universal and permanent action, carried out under the supreme authority of the IOC, of all individuals and entities who are inspired by the values of Olympism. It covers the five continents. It reaches its

> peak with the bringing together of the world's athletes at the great sports festival, the Olympic Games. Its symbol is five interlaced rings.

We could call this a political ideal, but the fifth Fundamental Principle of Olympism demands political neutrality. Rather, it aims to transcend political conflicts between governments by bringing ordinary people from different nations together to interact peacefully through sport.

The community ideal of international friendship is embedded in the Olympic symbol of five interlaced rings. Just as the Fundamental Principles of Olympism function as a corporate philosophy for the Olympic Movement, the interlocking rings function as a corporate logo. The rings are among the most commercially valuable symbols in the world, but as the economist Holger Preuss observes, that value derives from Olympic philosophy and the desire of brands and consumers to be associated with it.

According to the Charter, the Olympic symbol "expresses the activity of the Olympic Movement and represents the union of the five continents and the meeting of athletes from throughout the world at the Olympic Games." Indeed, the Games are the primary means by which the Movement pursues its community goal of a "peaceful society concerned with the preservation of human dignity." This is not a matter of government negotiations, however. Rather, the Olympic Movement uses sport to generate international interactions that promote moral dispositions conducive to peace.

Olympism seeks to create an international community based on shared humanity and common ideals. The Games themselves provide a temporary model of Olympism's community ideal by demonstrating peaceful interaction among people from diverse nations in a spirit of joy and friendship. The Charter states explicitly that the primary method for "building a peaceful and better world" is "educating youth through sport practiced in accordance with Olympism and its values."

The community ideal of Olympic friendship builds upon the personal and interpersonal dispositions cultivated through sport—especially the respect that transcends social differences. However, it focuses on groups, especially nations, and the power of sport to bring people together in a way that transcends political differences without erasing national distinctions.

Paradox: nationalism versus internationalism

This community ideal raises a final paradox. How can global peace and harmony be promoted by competition among national teams? Some say that international sports competitions only lead to hatred, and staging a festival among nations that have a past, present, or potential future of political and military conflict hardly seems like an effective way to prevent it.

Even idealists who regard peace as a reasonable goal despite its practical impossibility may question the use of national teams, flags, and anthems in the Olympic Games. Wouldn't it be better to cultivate international friendship by having all athletes compete under the Olympic Flag, perhaps identifying teams by sponsors as they do in professional leagues, or even by basic colors as they did in ancient Rome?

And what about the medal tables, which claim to determine which nation "wins" the Olympic Games? Rule six of the Olympic Charter states explicitly that, "The Olympic Games are competitions between athletes in individual or team events and not between countries." Nevertheless, the IOC, and almost every affiliated organization, publishes a medal table with a competitive ranking of countries on its official website.

A closer look reveals that Olympism's vision of global unity is compatible with and even served by international sport. Contrary to popular belief, Coubertin argued that nationalistic feelings need not be detrimental;

rather, bringing diverse national "peculiarities" into contact can foster a positive sense of pride in them (1901). Just as competition between athletes paradoxically dissipates their differences and emphasizes instead their common humanity, competition among nations helps to transcend the "us versus them" mentality generated by geopolitical conflicts and emphasize, instead, the collective "we."

Significantly, the Olympic Games are hosted by cities, not nations, and during the Games, individual people and individual nations are considered equally. Also, in international sports tournaments, national teams compete as equals with the same number of players given the same opportunities to perform. But the pseudo-contest imagined by the medal table fails that standard because national Olympic teams are comprised of different numbers of athletes competing in different types of events. Wealthier and more populous countries have a significant advantage. There isn't even a standard way to tally the rankings: some count the number of golds, others count total medals; apparently, choosing the method that favors their country.

The Olympic Games include several sports in which national teams compete in fair conditions, but the Games themselves are *not* a competition among nations. Rather, they are a way of bringing people from around the world together to acknowledge national distinctions on a cultural level while setting aside political differences for the sake of celebrating our common humanity. Though national uniforms, flags, and symbols are also associated with war, and athletic competition sometimes produces nationalistic emotions reminiscent of war, the motivations for organizing and competing in the Games are completely different.

Athletes are representatives of their nations, not instruments of their respective governments' will. Nations in this context are understood as groups of people united by a shared identity linked with a particular culture and territory—to celebrate a national team is to celebrate that group of people, not their government. In some ways, the display of national symbols at the Games serves to replace the paradigm of war with a spectacle of international competition between people and not armies; between friends and not foes.

Ancient Greek *ekecheiera*

It is noteworthy that the Ancient Greek Olympic Games were called *agōnes,* a term that designates not only contests, but also the public nature of such events—their ability to bring people together. The term *agōn* also refers to the site of a gathering and to the assembly of people (athletes, trainers, officials, spectators) collected there. So, it is important when we think about the Olympic Games, ancient or modern, to think not just about the sports themselves but about all the people involved in the event, and especially about the larger sense of community generated by the event.

It is easy to forget that there was no country of Greece in ancient times; the diverse groups of people brought together in Olympia were politically distinct entities linked primarily by language and religion. According to classical scholar Thomas Heine Nielsen, it was festivals like the Olympic Games that actually generated the concept of "Greeks" as a single nation of people. Such gatherings offered an opportunity to exercise the shared tradition of *xenia*—welcoming strangers without knowing who they are or where they come from—which clears space for the seeds of friendship to grow.

These festivals contrasted starkly with daily life since, despite the tradition of *xenia,* Greek city-states were in an almost constant state of rivalry and war. In fact, a religious protection for travelers called *ekecheiera* (literally "hands-off") was required to ensure diverse participation. The *ekecheiria* did not stop wars, but it created a time and space within which people's commonalities took precedence over their political differences.

As it turns out, the "safe space" provided by the Games not only served the purpose of worshipping common gods, but Olympia became a convenient site for peace negotiations and treaties. Over time, the Greek people discovered that they had enough in common to identify as a single community, and a shared cultural identity was formed. Even after their political independence was lost to the Roman Empire, athletics and the Olympic Games remained part of Greek identity. In fact, gymnasia and Olympic-style sport became a way to express "Greekness" even for people who weren't originally Greek.

The concept of a community that transcends political conflict was embraced and expanded by philosophers of the Roman Empire, including the Emperor Marcus Aurelius, who embraced the idea of cosmopolitanism attributed to Diogenes of Sinope in the 5th century BCE. "Cosmopolitan" means "citizen of the world," but as Marcus Aurelius explains, being a citizen of the world does not prevent me from also being a citizen of my country, a resident of my city, and a member of my family.

In other words, multiple identities can and do co-exist, as does responsible membership in multiple communities. It is a matter of how we think of ourselves. Being cosmopolitan means thinking of and treating other people from around the world as "fellow citizens" with equal rights and duties to our shared world. Like the *ekecheiria,* it does not stop wars or resolve political conflicts, but it sets them aside temporarily for the sake of affirming our common humanity. We may think of the Olympic Games as a model of such ideas.

Modern Olympic friendship

The truce that made the ancient Olympic Games possible was especially inspirational for Coubertin because, as historian John Hoberman notes, his ideas were shaped by a European *fin de siècle* internationalism that also inspired the creation of organizations dedicated to peacemaking, such as the International Red Cross, the Esperanto Movement, and the Scouting Movement. Coubertin saw truce as an essential element of Olympism's aim to keep positive national feelings from degrading into enmity. He understood, however, that the Olympic Games could not directly bring about world peace. Rather, the practical effect of the Games was to foster friendship among people from different nations.

Bringing together people from diverse social, cultural, ethnic, and political backgrounds was essential to this plan since Coubertin thought it would be impossible for them to cultivate mutual respect without meeting in person. "To ask the peoples of the world to love one another is no more than a sort of childishness," he said. "To ask them to respect one another is not an *idle* dream; but before they can esteem one another, they must first get to know one another" (1935).

Perhaps it was during his 1890 trip to the United States that Coubertin realized the moral harm caused by keeping people separate based on superficial differences. In his book, *Transatlantic Universities,* he recounts witnessing a black woman being forcibly removed from a train and placed in a dirty and uncomfortable "Negro car." Separation, thought Coubertin, widens human divisions and entrenches inequalities. Education, therefore, should be something that unites; a project that brings people together on a common ground. The Games would "provide a happy and fraternal meeting place for the youth of the world, a place where, gradually, the ignorance of each other in which people live will disappear" (1894).

Philosopher William J. Morgan sees in the Olympic project a possibility to get in contact with and learn the beliefs, values, and forms of life of others—which are prerequisites to treating them with moral discernment and respect, in the way they ought to be treated. In other words, Olympism's community ideal rejects separation and facilitates interactions that provide opportunities to overcome cultural, ethnic, and political prejudices.

Olympic friendship, therefore, is not to be understood in the ordinary sense of interpersonal affection. Rather, it is a moral disposition that arises from encountering others in an international sports festival. It does not require close connections or intimacy; it is based on the acknowledgement of others' humanity, and respectful interaction despite national differences. Coubertin hoped that international encounters would replace negative nationalism grounded in ignorance with a positive form based on understanding.

Parallel to the interpersonal respect generated within sport, Coubertin imagined international understanding to be generated among the diverse people gathered at the festival, whether working in supporting roles or enjoying the competitions as spectators. He thought Olympic internationalism would express "a state of mind among those who love their country above all, who seek to draw to it the friendship of foreigners by professing for the countries of those foreigners an intelligent and enlightened sympathy" (1898). In this way, Olympism would be "a destroyer of dividing walls" (1918), and the spectacle of the Olympic Games would create a model of community capable of making that goal of world peace at least seem possible.

How sport inspires international friendship

Besides cultivating excellence and respect, Coubertin asserted in 1918 that "sport can do something more for us," arguing specifically that it can safeguard the essential good of peace. Similar to Olympia's ancient sanctuary, he envisioned Olympic peace as a neutral, sportive atmosphere free from political conflicts and open to interaction among diverse peoples. He expressed this in his 1912 *Ode to Sport*:

> [Sport] You forge happy bonds between the people by drawing them together in reverence for strength [...]. Through you, the young of all the world learn to respect one another, and thus the diversity of national traits becomes a source of generous, peaceful emulation.

In other words, sports can foster international friendship by revealing the compatibility of group identities. Kretchmar argues that sports generate their own group identities based on common interest in the practice. In these communities, national and political differences are set aside as people claim a common identity as judokas, divers, rowers, and so on, forming friendly bonds grounded in their shared commitment to the practice.

In his analysis of the relationship between sport and democracy, Paul Christesen likewise observed that the bonding power of sport originates from the fact that sports function as social networks that require repeated, cooperative interactions guided by norms, and that, even in opposition, individuals share common objectives. For him, the bonding generated by sport extends beyond the contest, fostering solidarity and creating trust among people who would not normally interact.

Sociologist Richard Giulianotti confirms that when individuals share significant experiences marked by a heightened sense of collective emotion, they develop bonds of unity and solidarity. These effects emerge in concerts, religious festivals, and, of course, international sports gatherings like the Olympic Games—for athletes, coaches, fans, volunteers, media, and staff alike. In other words, all those present at the event contribute to shaping this collective bond. This helps to explain why, at the Games, we see fans from different nations cheer for one another or show empathy when athletes from another country lose: they are immersed in an atmosphere of unity and solidarity that derives from sports' communal identities.

The international friendship that Olympism envisions is based on unity and solidarity, which is nurtured both by identities generated from our common interest in sport and by the bonds generated within the practice itself. This aligns with philosopher Irena Martínková's claim that the kind of international interactions facilitated by the Olympic Games are ethically significant. Facilitating face-to-face encounters with others, especially those who are different, helps us to overcome ignorance and fear, and makes it difficult to sustain negative feelings. It is a process that gradually transforms strangers into familiar others.

Thus, the community ideal of international friendship in Olympism is not a political peace mission, but rather the promotion of unity, solidarity, mutual understanding, and recognition of shared humanity. It sets aside political conflicts to celebrate national and cultural characteristics. As Lenk argues, the ideals of Olympism expressed in the Olympic Games offer "a symbol of a better world, an understanding among the sports youth crossing all national and cultural boundaries."

The Olympic flag

The Olympic flag effectively symbolizes the ideal of international friendship through sport. According to the Olympic Charter,

> In 1914, the Olympic flag presented by Pierre de Coubertin at the Paris Congress was adopted. It includes the five interlaced rings, which represent the union of the five continents and the meeting of athletes from throughout the world at the Olympic Games.

From the start, the ideals behind the symbol were challenged by reality. Anthropologist Susan Brownell recounts Coubertin asking, "Are these five rings solidly riveted together? Will war someday shatter the framework?" As a matter of fact, World War I broke out the same year, and it wasn't until Antwerp in 1920 that the flag would fly over the Games. An original flag from Antwerp was ceremonially passed between summer Olympic hosts until 1988, when it was retired. However, the ritual of passing the Olympic flag to the next city remains an important part of the Closing Ceremony.

Symbols give meaning to rituals, and what the Olympic flag stands for should not be forgotten. The five equal interlaced rings represent world unity, but the colors of those rings, combined with the white background, represent all the national flags in the world. So, the flag represents unity *and* diversity, or perhaps the unity that emerges from diversity, the process of gathering together for the Games. It is through the competitive "interlocking" of the athletes representing their nations that international friendship is cultivated.

If nothing else, the competition between athletes or teams wearing their national colors reminds us that nations can also compete outside of sport in a mutually beneficial way. White, meanwhile, is a traditional color of peace, or at least temporary truce, as in raising a white flag in battle. Just as white forms the background for the interlocking rings on the Olympic flag, truce forms the background for the more peaceful world it seeks to bring about.

The emotional power of the opening and closing ceremonies, along with the Olympic flag, is used in the Games to promote the idea of international friendship. Rule 53 of the Olympic Charter states that "an Olympic flag of larger dimensions than any other flag must fly for the entire duration of the Olympic Games from a flagpole placed in a prominent position," but this does not discourage the presence of national flags. Indeed, athletes competing independently or as refugees march under the Olympic flag, without renouncing their nationality.

The ideal of international friendship imagines an Olympic community based on shared values that coexists with national identities. Nationalism, understood as an inclusive concept that also respects foreigners, is to be distinguished from exclusive forms of pride that reject or diminish everyone outside of the group. The Olympic flag represents a community of friendship that includes individuals and nations alike.

Critics and challenges

Even though Olympism aims to promote a peaceful society through international sport, critics say the Olympic Movement has not only failed to nurture this sentiment but actually reinforces hostilities among people from different nations. While the Charter claims that Olympic competition is between athletes rather than countries, historian William Murray maintains that, in practice, the Games have become a battlefield of "nations trying to crush one another." Another historian, Douglas Booth, observes that historical and political rivalries are played out in the sporting arena, transforming the Games into a stage where nations seek to symbolically vanquish adversaries.

Indeed, the infamous "Blood in the Water Match" between Hungary and the USSR at the 1956 Games achieved the opposite of Coubertin's desire that nationalistic sentiments should be "temporarily dismissed" (1935). For many, friendship and peace can never be achieved through athletic competitions, since, to use Orwell's words, "international sport is bound up with hatred, jealousy, and violence." However, the presence of negative examples does not strictly imply that the philosophy of Olympism is flawed or that its goals are impossible to achieve.

Some might suggest that the Olympic Movement could avoid negative nationalism by eliminating national teams, but creating a spectacle of peaceful interaction among nations seems to require them. Perhaps, it is enough to recall that the prefix *inter* means "between" or "among," as in *intermingle, interaction,* or *intertwine;* it does not imply opposition. In fact, the YOG have introduced events that allow athletes from different and even warring nations to compete together as teammates, an experience that often sparks feelings of friendship. These innovations align with Coubertin's aspirations, since they provide individuals from diverse backgrounds to meet and collaborate towards a common goal.

Notably, there is no medal table in the YOG, implicitly suggesting that the "medal competition" is irrelevant to the objectives of Olympism. Yet, such practices should become the general model for structuring competitions within the Olympic Movement and not be limited only to the youth. By grounding the organization of the Games in the ideals of Olympism, the Movement can counteract the negative nationalism often cultivated in the media, which tends to fuel a hostile environment in the field of play and discourage unity.

The political exploitation of Olympic events is sometimes evident even before competitions begin. One of the most troubling examples occurs when athletes decline to compete against opponents from a politically or militarily adversarial state. Even more striking are cases in which teams refuse to share the same transportation with representatives of such states. These actions clearly contradict the Olympic ideal of international friendship. Yet other, more "normalized" practices likewise reduce opportunities for connection rather than unity. Athletes are typically grouped by nation in the Olympic Village and during the Opening

Ceremony, but they could be grouped by sport instead, or prescriptively mixed together.

The YOG have introduced a variety of activities that encourage interaction beyond competition, providing opportunities to meet and get to know one another. In the opening ceremony of the 2018 Buenos Aires YOG, for example, all athletes marched together, not separated by country. Also, cultural and educational programs allow athletes to engage in activities related to community, arts, and culture, as well as initiatives that teach about social responsibility, well-being, and healthy lifestyles.

Beyond the specific objectives of these activities, the broader goal is to create an environment where athletes can interact with representatives from different countries, share cultural experiences, and develop relationships that cultivate Olympism's ideal of international friendship. Replicating these practices in the Olympic Games could contribute to this ideal and prevent the Games from acting against their own interests by failing to foster maximum interaction among participants.

Conclusion

In 1956, an Australian teenager named John Ian Wing wrote an anonymous letter to the IOC suggesting that athletes mix together in the closing ceremony of the Melbourne Games, rather than marching as separate teams. The proposal was adopted and has been followed ever since, modeling the ideal of international friendship even after the Olympic flame is extinguished. As with the other ideals, this is only symbolic, and it is telling that the different national teams tend to stick together despite being free to mix with the others.

The ideal of international friendship represented by the Olympic flag is elusive, which is exactly why we need to work toward it by adopting that disposition in our daily lives. On the other hand, we can see that Olympism's ideals have power. They give the rings their communal value, sport its interpersonal value, and athletes a special personal value. Olympism's ideals are what make these athletes, sports, and rings truly "Olympic."

Questions for reflection and discussion

1. Have you seen countries foster hostile attitudes toward athletes or teams from other nations? If so, how might Olympic institutions help diminish these negative sentiments and promote international friendship among competitors?
2. Even though Olympism seeks to encourage interaction among participants off the field of

play, this rarely happens. What initiatives might you propose to your NOC that would foster such international interaction?

References

Booth, D. (2004). Post-Olympism? Questioning Olympic Historiography. In J. Bale & M. Christensen (Eds.), *Post Olympism? Questioning Sport in the Twenty-first Century* (pp. 13-32). Berg.

Brownell, S. (2024). The Olympic symbols and ceremonies. *Olympic Knowledge Essential Readings Series* online.

Coubertin, P. (1890). Louisiana, Florida, and Virginia. In N. Müller ed. 2000 (pp. 95-96).

Coubertin, P. (1894). The Neo-Olympism. Appeal to the people of Athens. In N. Müller ed. 2000 (pp. 533-541).

Coubertin, P. (1898). Does cosmopolitan life lead to international friendliness? *American Monthly Review of Reviews, 17*, 429-434.

Coubertin, P. (1901). *Notes sur l'éducation publique*. Hachette.

Coubertin, P. (1912). Ode to Sport. In N. Müller ed. 2000 (pp. 629-630).

Coubertin, P. (1918). Olympic Letter III: Olympism and Education. In N. Müller ed. 2000 (pp. 547-548).

Coubertin, P. (1918). What we can now ask of sport. Address given to the Greek liberal club of Lausanne. In N. Müller ed. 2000 (pp. 269-277).

Coubertin, P. (1935). The Fundamentals of the Philosophy of the Modern Olympics. *Olympic Review* 56 (1956), 52-54.

Christesen, P. (2012). *Sport and democracy in the ancient and modern worlds*. Cambridge University Press.

Giulianotti, R. (2016). *Sport: A Critical Sociology*. John Wiley & Sons.

Hoberman, J. (1995). Toward a theory of Olympic internationalism. *Journal of Sport History*, 22(1), 1-37.

Kretchmar, R. S. (2018). The nature and value of sporting tests and contests. *NYLS Law Review*, *63*(2), 219 - 233.

Lenk, H. (1982). Tasks of the Philosophy of Sport: Between Publicity and Anthropology. *Journal of the Philosophy of Sport*, *9*(1), 94-106.

Martínková, I. (2012). Pierre de Coubertin's vision of the role of sport in peaceful internationalism. *Sport in Society*, *15*(6), 788-97.

Murray, W.J. (1992). France, Coubertin and the Nazi Olympics: The Response. *Olympika: The International Journal of Olympic Studies* 1(1), 46-69.

Morgan, W. J. (1994). Coubertin's theory of Olympic internationalism: A critical reinterpretation. In *Critical Reflections on Olympic Ideology: Second International Symposium for Olympic Research* (pp. 10-25).

Nielsen, T.H. (2024) "A Brief Essay on Sport and Greek Unity in the Late Archaic and Early Classical Period." *Classica Et Mediaevalia,* (1), 67–90.

Orwell, G. (1945). The Sporting Spirit. *Tribune* 468(14), 10-11.

Preuss, H. (2000). The Economics of the Olympic Games: Hosting the Games 1982-2000. Walla Walla Press.

Conclusion

Ideals Matter

Those who write about ideal societies are often criticized for advocating impractical and unrealistic visions detached from social reality. This book, however, has not neglected the historical realities of the modern Olympic Games. On the contrary, it has shown that Olympic history is marked by numerous events that conflict with their ideals. Yet, we have argued that the commitment and obligation to improve the realities of the Movement arise precisely from the ideals and values articulated in the Fundamental Principles of Olympism.

The Olympic ideals visible in the practice of sport today were present in Ancient Greek thought and brought back to life the by modern revival. Even if it may be difficult to fully comprehend Olympic ideals, they are neither naïve nor irrelevant. They are worth defending not only because they provide the foundation and purpose of the Olympic Movement, but especially because ideals are what make the Games Olympic.

We acknowledge that Olympic ideals are often disrespected in practice. When, for example, athletes cheat or exploit competitive advantages unavailable to others, they undermine the ideal of Olympic excellence. But athletes are not solely or even primarily responsible for supporting the ideals. When Olympic institutions create environments that prioritize outcomes—medals, records, and financial returns—over moral growth, they do systematic damage to the Movement.

In the interpersonal dimension, a "winning at all costs" attitude undermines the mutual improvement sport is meant to foster. Institutions sustain and amplify this attitude by pushing for medals and records, but such approaches tend to disregard fair play and diminish Olympic respect. Finally, organizers who fail to create spaces for meaningful interaction between athletes, like media narratives that frame nations as enemies, further distance the Movement from its community ideal of international friendship.

Such challenges can be addressed effectively only if those within the Olympic Movement seriously engage with the meaning of Olympism and its ideals. In other words, Olympic practices and realities must be constantly scrutinized and evaluated in light of the values that underpin the Movement. Reflection on Olympic ideals makes clear that the Movement and Games are not concerned with medals, records, or profit (as many seem to think), but rather with fostering morally and socially valuable dispositions at the personal, interpersonal, and community levels.

Understanding Olympic ideals includes the realization that meaningful change depends on us—on the way we act within the Olympic Movement, but also on our approach to daily life. Paradoxically, Olympism and its values can flourish only if people quit viewing the Olympic Games as a site for personal gain or national domination, and begin to understand them as a project grounded in ideals and oriented toward social and moral improvement. Olympic ideals matter because they stretch our interpretative horizons: they enable us to recognize what has been lost or neglected, and they provide the resources needed to reanimate and reorient Olympic reality toward its enduring ideals.

Appendix of Resources for Olympic Studies

Glossary of Greek Terms

Aidōs (αἰδώς): is a moral feeling of reverence that generates respectful behavior. It can take the form of awe with regard to gods and heroes, compassion for to those in need, or honor and shame with regard to one's own conscience.

Agōn (ἀγών): denotes an assembly of spectators and contestants gathered for a competition, including sports, drama, trials, and even war. The Olympics are referred to even in modern Greek as *agōnes* and not "games."

Aretē (ἀρετή): is the quality that makes anything excellent in its kind. Sport was thought to reveal and celebrate human *aretē,* which showed our closeness to heroes and gods. In philosophy, *aretē* was a moral condition that enabled good action, similar to what we call "character."

Athlos (ἆθλος) plural *athloi*: feat, ordeal, contest, or labor like those performed by Heracles (see also *ponos*). An "athlete" is one who performs an *athlos,* not necessarily in sport.

Ekecheiria (ἐκεχειρία): cessation of hostilities or truce; literally "hands off." The ancient Olympic truce was originally a protection for pilgrims travelling to the festival; it did not stop wars.

Ponos (πόνος), plural *ponoi*: the labor, effort, or toil required to achieve *athloi*. Heracles' "labors" are called *ponoi* and Socrates uses that term to describe his philosophical "service" to the city of Athens in Plato's *Apology*.

Xenia (ξενία): a sacred bond of hospitality in which the host is expected to welcome the stranger (*xenos*) and provide for him without knowing his name or purpose.

The Olympic Anthem
by Kostis Palamas
(*Source: IOC official website*)

"O Ancient immortal Spirit, pure father
Of beauty, of greatness and of truth,
Descend, reveal yourself and flash like lightning here,
within the glory of your own earth and sky.

At running and at wrestling and at throwing,
Shine in the momentum of noble contests,
And crown with the unfading branch
And make the body worthy and ironlike.

Plains, mountains and seas glow with you
Like a white-and-purple great temple,
And hurries at the temple here, your pilgrim,
O Ancient immortal Spirit, every nation."

Invocation
for the Lighting of the Olympic Flame

(Source: Hellenic Olympic Committee official website)

Sacred silence
Let the sky, the earth, the sea and the winds sound.
Mountains fall silent.
Sounds and birds' warbles cease.
For Phoebus, the Light bearer King shall keep us company.

Apollo God of sun and the idea of light
send your rays and light the sacred torch
for the hospitable city of…[host city]
And you Zeus give peace to all peoples on earth and wreath the winners
of the Sacred Race

Olympic Oath

(Source: IOC official website)

We promise to take part in these Olympic Games, respecting and abiding by the rules and in the spirit of fair play, inclusion and equality. Together we stand in solidarity and commit ourselves to sport without doping, without cheating, without any form of discrimination. We do this for the honor of our teams, in respect for the Fundamental Principles of Olympism, and to make the world a better place through sport.

Electronic Databases

Scholars in Olympic Studies are fortunate to have a wide variety of resources available free online.

CEO-UAB Digital Document Collection
https://ddd.uab.cat/collection/ceo?ln=en

International Olympic Academy Articles and Publications https://www.ioa.org.gr/the-academy/articles-publications

International Pierre de Coubertin Committee Publications https://www.coubertin.org/academic-activities/publications/

Journal of Olympic Studies
https://olympicstudies.org/

LA84 Foundation Digital Library
https://digital.la84.org/digital

Olympic Knowledge – Essential Reading Series
https://library.olympics.com/default/essential-readings.aspx?_lg=en-GB

Olympic World Library
https://library.olympics.com/

Olympics.com Documents
https://www.olympics.com/ioc/documents

Annotated Bibliography

The following list of resources, which we do not take to be exhaustive, are recommended for research or development of courses in Olympic studies.

Books

Bale, J., & Christensen, M.K. (Eds.). (2020). *Post-Olympism: Questioning Sport in the Twenty-first Century*. Routledge. A collection of essays criticizing Olympism and the Olympic Games.

Barringer, J.M. (2021) *Olympia. A Cultural history,* Princeton. A foundational reading on the archaeological site and its history.

Bernand, A. (2003). *The Road to Olympia: Origins of the Olympic Games*. Periplus. An illustrated account of the ancient Games.

Cebrián, R.B. (2020). *The Athlete in the Ancient Greek World.* University of Oklahoma Press. An attempt to reconstruct the experience of ancient athletes using a variety of evidence.

Christesen, P. & Kyle, D.G. (Eds). (2014) *A Companion to Sport and Spectacle in Greek and Roman antiquity.* Wiley. A variety of essays on almost every aspect of ancient athletics.

Crowther, N.B. (2004). *Athletika: Studies on the Olympic Games and Greek Athletics.* Hildesheim: Weidmann. A collection of short articles on various aspects of ancient athletics and the Olympic Games.

Da Costa, L. (Ed.). (2002). *Olympic Studies - Current Intellectual Crossroads*. Editora Gama Filho. A collection of diverse perspectives on the Olympic Games and its philosophy.

Drees, L. (1968). *Olympia: Gods, Artists and Athletes*. Praeger. An account of the ancient Olympic Games that focuses on their religious origin.

Espy, R. (1981). *The Politics of the Olympic Games*. University of California Press. Explores the post-war relationship between the Olympic Games and international politics.

Finley, M.I. & H.W. Pleket (1976). *The Olympic Games: The First Thousand Years*. Chatto-Windhus. A highly readable and relevant history of the ancient Games, once the standard text.

Georgiadis, K. (2003). *Olympic Revival: The Revival of the Olympic Games in Modern Times*. Athenon. A perceptive and detailed history of the modern revival written by the dean of the IOA.

Golden, M. (2008). *Greek Sport and Social Status*. University of Texas Press. An insightful analysis of ancient Greek athletics from the perspective of social class.

Guttmann, A. (1978). *From Ritual to Record: The nature of modern sports*. Columbia University Press. A socio-historical analysis sport's evolution from antiquity to modern times.

Guttmann, A. (2002). *The Olympics: a history of the modern games*. University of Illinois Press. A look at political issues in the Olympic Games from the revival to the end of the millennium.

König, J. (Ed.) (2010). *Greek Athletics*. Edinburgh University Press. Essays on sport in ancient Greece from gymnastics to identity.

Lenk, H. (2024). *Rowing Home To Old Olympia*. Projekt. Reflections from an Olympic gold medalist and professional philosopher on the meaning of Olympia.

Lenskyj, H. (2000). *Inside the Olympic Industry: Power, Politics, and Activism*. SUNY. A social critique of the modern Games.

Lenskyj, H., & Wagg, S. (Eds.). (2012). *The Palgrave handbook of Olympic studies*. Palgrave. Essays on social issues such as race, gender, and commercialization.

Lunt, D. (2022). *The Crown Games of Ancient Greece: archaeology, athletes, and heroes*. University of Arkansas Press. An account of the Panhellenic Games that considers their cultural context.

MacAloon, J.J. (2013). *This Great Symbol: Pierre de Coubertin and the origins of the modern Olympic Games*. Routledge. A historical/ anthropological analysis of the Olympic revival and its connection to ritual and symbol.

Miller, P.J. (2022). *Sport: Antiquity and its Legacy.* Bloomsbury. A recent book linking various aspects of ancient and modern sport, including the ancient and modern Olympic Games.

Miller, S.G. (2004). *Ancient Greek athletics*. Yale University Press. A well-organized and readable account of ancient Greek athletics that explores its archaeology in cultural context.

Mitsopoulou, C., Farnoux, A., & Jeammet, V. (Eds.). (2024). *L'Olympisme, une invention moderne, un héritage antique*. Louvre Éditions. Catalog of an exhibition for the 2024 Olympic Games.

Müller, N. (2000). *Pierre de Coubertin 1863-1937 - Olympism: Selected Writings.* IOC. Contains Coubertin's key writings in the development of Olympism and the Olympic Games, translated into English.

Neils, J. (2004). *Striving for Excellence: ancient Greek childhood and the Olympic spirit.* Alexander S. Onasis Public Benefit Foundation. A short book that combines essays about children and young athletes with athletic images.

Nielsen, T.H. (2004). *Use and Abuse of the Ancient Olympics by Classical Greek City-states.* Weidmann. An exploration of the political motives for participating in the ancient Games.

Potter, D. (2011). *Victor's Crown: A History of Ancient Sport from Homer to Byzantium.* Oxford University Press. Contains interesting chapters suitable for further reading.

Reid, H.L. (2024). *Ancient Olympic Philosophy: Sport, Athletes, Excellence, Women, Beauty, Fairness, Peace.* Parnassos Press. Essays on philosophical topics from the ancient Olympic Games.

Reid, H.L. (2020). *Olympic Philosophy: the ideas and ideals behind the ancient and modern Olympic Games.* Parnassos Press. Scholarly essays on the philosophical ideas that underpin the Games.

Reid, H.L. (2011). *Athletics and Philosophy in the Ancient World: Contests of Virtue.* Routledge. Essays connecting philosophy and athletic practice in ancient Greece and Rome.

Reid, H.L., & Austin, M.W. (Eds.). (2012). *The Olympics and Philosophy.* University Press of Kentucky. Scholarly essays on philosophical issues surrounding the modern Games.

Remijsen, S. (2015). *The End of Greek Athletics in Late Antiquity.* Cambridge University Press. Covers the demise of Greek athletics in late antiquity from the perspectives of sport, religion, and politics.

Segrave, J., & Chu, D. (Eds.). (1981). *Olympism.* Human Kinetics Publishers. Scholarly essays on the origins, philosophy, and politics of the modern Games.

Smith, M.L. (2004). *The Olympics in Athens 1896: the invention of the modern Olympic Games.* Profile Books. A history of the Olympic revival and its connection to the excavations at Ancient Olympia.

Spaaij, R., & Burleson, C. (Eds.). (2016). *The Olympic Movement and the Sport of Peacemaking*. Routledge. A collection of essays about the social impact of the Olympic Movement and peacemaking efforts through sport.

Spivey, N. (2004). *The Ancient Olympics.* Oxford University Press. A short, readable history of the ancient Olympics that takes into account their connection to the modern revival.

Stocking, C.H. & Stephens, S.A. (2021). *Ancient Greek Athletics: primary sources in translation.* Oxford University Press. A treasure trove of ancient sources in translation with helpful explanatory essays.

Swaddling, J. (2015). *The Ancient Olympic Games.* University of Texas Press. A basic introduction to the ancient Olympic Games written for the general public with emphasis on art and aesthetics, lavishly illustrated.

Tyrrell, W.B. (2004). *The Smell of Sweat: Greek athletics, Olympics, and culture.* Bolchazy-Carducci Publishers. A source book tracing ancient Greek athletics from Homer to the Olympic Games, covering myths, events, and other athletic festivals such as the Panathenian Games.

Waterfield, R. (2018). *Olympia: the story of the ancient Olympic Games*. Bloomsbury. Exposes the reality of the ancient Olympic Games by exploring the purposes, politics and rituals surrounding them.

Young, D.C. (2002). *The Modern Olympics: A struggle for revival*. Johns Hopkins University Press. A historical reconstruction of the revival of the modern Olympic Games in the 19th century with attention to their ancient heritage.

Young, D.C. (1984). *The Olympic Myth of Greek Amateur Athletics*. Ares Press. Exposes how erroneous understanding of ancient sports were used to validate modern sport ideologies.

Articles

Aggerholm, K. (2025). Sport humanism: Contours of a humanist theory of sport. *Journal of the Philosophy of Sport, 52*(1), 1-24.

Arnold, P.J. (1996). Olympism, Sport, and Education. *Quest, 48*(1), 93-101.

Arnold, P.J. (1994). Sport and moral education. *Journal of moral education, 23*(1), 75-89.

Barney, R., & Bijkerk, A. (2005). The Genesis of Sacred Fire in Olympic Ceremony. *Journal of Olympic History, 13*(2), 6-27.

Butcher, R., & Schneider, A. (1998). Fair play as respect for the game. *Journal of the Philosophy of Sport*, *25*(1), 1-22.

Da Costa, L. (2006). A Never-Ending Story: The Philosophical Controversy Over Olympism. *Journal of the Philosophy of Sport* *33*(2), 157-73.

Gleaves, J., & Llewellyn, M. (2014). Ethics, nationalism, and the imagined community: The case against inter-national sport. *Journal of the Philosophy of Sport*, *41*(1), 1-19.

Hoberman, J. (1995). Toward a theory of Olympic internationalism. *Journal of Sport History*, 22(1), 1-37.

Holowchak, M.A. (2011). The "Measure" of an Athletic Achievement Character versus Production, or a Forced Dichotomy in Competitive Sport. *Journal of the Philosophy of Sport*, *38*(1), 88-102.

Hyland, D. (1977). "And That Is The Best Part of Us:" Human Beings and Play. *Journal of the Philosophy of Sport*, 4(1), 36-49.

Jirásek, I. (2015). Religion, Spirituality, and Sport: From *Religio Athletae* Toward *Spiritus Athletae*. *Quest*, *67*(3), 290–299.

Loland, S. (2002). The logic of progress and the art of moderation in competitive sports. In C. Tamburrini & T. Tannsjo (Eds.), *Values in Sport* (pp. 49-68). Taylor & Francis.

Lenk, H. (1982). Tasks of the Philosophy of Sport: Between Publicity and Anthropology. *Journal of the Philosophy of Sport, 9*(1), 94-106.

Martínková, I. (2012). Pierre de Coubertin's vision of the role of sport in peaceful internationalism. *Sport in Society, 15*(6), 788-97.

Martínková, I. (2012). Fair or Temple: Two Possibilities for Olympic Sport. *Sport, Ethics and Philosophy, 6*(2), 166-182.

McNamee, M. (2006). Olympism, Eurocentricity, and Transcultural Virtues. *Journal of the Philosophy of Sport, 33*(2), 174-187.

Morgan, W.J. (1995). Cosmopolitanism, Olympism, and nationalism: A critical interpretation of Coubertin's ideal of international sporting life. *Olympika - London, Ontario, 4*, 79-92.

Parry, J. (2012). The power of sport in peacemaking and peacekeeping. *Sport in Society 15*(6), 775-87.

Parry, J. (2006). Sport and Olympism: Universals and multiculturalism. *Journal of the Philosophy of Sport, 33*(2), 188-204.

Reid, H.L. (2017). Why Olympia matters for modern sport. *Journal of the Philosophy of Sport, 44*(2), 159-173.

Reid, H.L. (2006). Olympic sport and its lessons for peace. *Journal of the Philosophy of Sport, 33*(2), 205-214.

Sailors, P.R., Teetzel, S., & Weaving, C. (2015). *Lentius, Inferius, Debilus*: the ethics of 'not trying' on the Olympic Stage. *Sport in Society, 18*(1), 17-27.

Shields, D., & Bredemeier, B. (2011). Contest, competition, and metaphor. *Journal of the Philosophy of Sport, 38*(1), 27-38.

Teetzel, S. (2012). Optimizing Olympic Education: a comprehensive approach to understanding and teaching the philosophy of Olympism. *Educational Review, 64*(3), 317-332.

Torres, C. (2006). Results or Participation? Reconsidering Olympism's Approach to Competition. *Quest, 58*(2), 242-54.

Journals in Olympic Studies

Diagoras: International Academic Journal on Olympic Studies ISSN 2565-196X

Journal of Olympic Studies (USA) ISSN 2639-6025

Journal of Olympic History (International) ISSN 3005-9720

Olympika: The International Journal for Olympic Studies (Canada) ISSN 1188-5963

Olimpianos: Journal of Olympic Studies (Brazil) ISSN 2526-6314.

Journals in the History and Philosophy of Sport

European Studies in Sports History (France) ISSN 1999-8589

Fairplay, Journal of Philosophy, Ethics and Sports Law (Spain) ISSN 2014-9255

Journal of the Philosophy of Sport (USA) ISSN 0094-8705

Journal of Sport History (USA) ISSN 0094-1700

Nikephoros (Germany) ISSN 0934-8913

Sport, Ethics and Philosophy (United Kingdom) ISSN 1751-1321

Stadion: International Journal of the history of Sport (Germany) ISSN 0172-4029

The International Journal of the History of Sport (United Kingdom) ISSN 0952-3367

About the Authors

Rafael Mendoza González, from Mexico, holds a PhD in Human Movement and Sport Sciences from the University of Rome "Foro Italico" and a Masters in Olympic Studies from the University of the Peloponnese. He focuses on the philosophy and sociology of sport, with emphasis on ethics, education, play theory, and Olympism. He has worked in the communications departments of sports organizations, including the International Paralympic Committee. His current research examines the relationship between sport and human rights, and the philosophical foundations of both the modern and ancient Olympic Games.

Heather L. Reid is Scholar in Residence at the Exedra Mediterranean Center in Siracusa, Sicily, and Professor Emerita at Morningside University in the USA. She is a 2015 Fellow of the American Academy in Rome, 2018-2020 Fellow of the Harvard Center for Hellenic Studies, and 2019 Fulbright Scholar at the Università degli Studi di Napoli Federico II. Her books include *Ancient Olympic Philosophy* (2024), *Olympic Philosophy* (2020), *Introduction to the Philosophy of Sport* (2012, 2nd ed. 2023), *Athletics and Philosophy in the Ancient World: Contests of Virtue* (2011), and *The Philosophical Athlete* (2002, 2nd ed. 2019).

www.ingramcontent.com/pod-product-compliance
Lightning Source LLC
La Vergne TN
LVHW091004080826
845145LV00003B/1127

9781942495819